MORE EVERYDAY CIRCLE TIMES

by

Liz & Dick Wilmes

art

DAVID JENSEN

A  Publication

38W567 Brindlewood, Elgin, Illinois 60123

ISBN 0-943452-14-7

ART

Cover Design and Art: David Van Delinder
STUDIO 155
Elgin, IL 60120

Text Illustrations: David Jensen

PUBLISHED BY:
BUILDING BLOCKS
38W567 Brindlewood
Elgin, IL 60123

DISTRIBUTED BY:
GRYPHON HOUSE
P.O. Box 275
Mt. Rainier, MD 20712

ISBN 0-943452-14-7

DEDICATED TO

...more young children who learn and grow everyday and to their teachers who stimulate and encourage this growth

Contents

Science

Occupations

Recreation

SCHOOL BEGINS

FOR OPENERS

BRING ONE OF YOUR FAVORITE PUPPETS TO CIRCLE TIME. HAVE THE PUPPET AND CHILDREN SING THE 'HELLO' SONG TOGETHER. AT THE END OF THE SONG POINT TO EACH CHILD AND LET HIM QUICKLY SING HOW HE FEELS.

HELLO

(TUNE: WHERE IS THUMBKIN?)

PUPPET SAYS: *WHERE ARE THE CHILDREN?*
WHERE ARE THE CHILDREN?

CHILDREN ANSWER: *HERE WE ARE! HERE WE ARE!*

PUPPET ASKS: *HOW ARE YOU TODAY, CHILDREN?*
HOW ARE YOU TODAY, CHILDREN?

EACH CHILD ANSWERS: *I AM FINE! (HAPPY, SAD, ANGRY, ETC.)*

FINGERPLAYS

GOOD MORNING
(tune: Happy Birthday)
Good morning to you,
Good morning to you,
Good morning everyone,
Good morning to you.

HAPPY DAY
(tune: Merrily We Roll Along)
We have had a happy day,
Happy day, happy day.
We have had a happy day,
We'll see you all tomorrow

SELF CONCEPT

SNACK

MORNING MUNCHIE

YOU'LL NEED

Pretzel sticks
Raisins
Carob chips
Sandwich bags

TO MAKE: Let the children pour and then mix all of the ingredients in a large bowl. Put a handful of the snack in each sandwich bag.

LANGUAGE GAMES

WE'RE ALL HERE Draw a giant gingerbread character on butcher paper. Cut it out. Bring it and a marker to circle time. Have each child say his/her name. As s/he does, write it on the character. When you're finished, ask the children where they would like you to hang `Mrs Gingerbread' after circle time.

I LIKE Give each child a large colored sticker to put on the back of his hand. Let him hold it up and call out what color sticker it is.
Tell the children to keep the stickers on. During the day, ask each child what he likes to do best at school. Draw a smile on each sticker and write, in one word, what activity each child named. Encourage the children to wear their stickers home and tell their families about school.

GOOD-BYE Just before going home, talk with the children about different non-verbal ways to say good-bye, such as a hug, handshake, high-5, or smile. Pick one of their suggestions, have them turn to the children near them and say good-bye. Then everyone sing `HAPPY DAY.' Repeat on other days using different non- verbal ways to say good-bye.

ACTIVE GAMES

FOLLOW THE LEADER

Before circle time, make the *'Morning Munchie'* snack. and choose a book to read to the children. Put them in a picnic basket. Hide the basket for later.

Have the children gather in a line behind you. Tell them to watch your actions as you all take a walk around the classroom and through the school. Begin the game by walking and waving your arms in the air. As you go around the classroom, stop at the different learning centers and talk to the children about the types of activities that they can do in each one. Continue the walk.

Near the end of the walk, come upon the picnic basket. Pick it up and carry it with you. When you return to the classroom, have the children sit around the basket. Open it up and see what is inside. Yes! A snack for each person and a book to read while having snack.

FRIENDSHIP WALK

Have all of the children sit in a circle. Choose a child. Turn on one of the children's favorite records. The child should begin to walk around the outside of the circle as the music plays. When you stop the music, the child should stop and hold hands with the child closest to him. Begin the music. Now the two children walk around the circle. Each time you stop the music, the children select the child they are closest to. That child joins their `Friendship Walk.' The game continues until all of the children are walking.

MY FAVORITE EXERCISE

Have the children stand in a group with room in the middle. Name a child. That child should go into the middle, tell the others what his favorite exercise is, and then lead all of them in it. After awhile say, *"Stop."* Name another child and let him tell and lead another exercise. Continue exercising.

BOOKS

MIRIAM COHEN — *BEST FRIENDS*
MIRIAM COHEN — *WILL I HAVE A FRIEND?*
TOMI DePAOLA — *BILL AND PETE*
MAXINE ROSENBERG — *MY FRIEND LESLIE, THE STORY OF A HANDICAPPED CHILD*

SELF CONCEPT

9

MY BODY

FOR OPENERS

DUPLICATE THE `KEEP YOUR BODY HEALTHY' CHART. GLUE IT TO A PIECE OF POSTER BOARD. TALK ABOUT HOW EACH OF THE CHILDREN IN THE PICTURES IS KEEPING HEALTHY. DO YOUR CHILDREN DO THAT ACTIVITY? WHEN AND HOW DO THEY DO IT?

FINGERPLAYS

CLAP YOUR HANDS

Clap your hands 1, 2, 3.
Clap your hands just like me.

Roll your hands 1, 2, 3.
Roll your hands just like me.

Continue with other movements.

STRETCH

I stretch and stretch and find it fun,
To reach and try to touch the sun.
I bend and bend to touch the floor,
'Til muscles in my legs get sore.

STOP

Clap your hands
And STOP your motion.
Turn around
And STOP your motion.
Touch your knees
And STOP your motion.
Everybody run, run, run around the mountain.
Run, run, run around the mountain.
Run, run, run around the mountain.
Everybody STOP.

(Continue, using other movements, slide, hop, etc.)

WHAT'S ON A FACE

Here's a face,
Now let's begin.
It has two ears,
A nose and chin.
A mouth, two eyes,
With a bushy brow.
What's on a face?
We all know now!
  Dick Wilmes

WIGGLE

Wiggle your fingers
Wiggle your toes
Reach for the ceiling
Touch your arms with your nose.

Stick out your arms
Wave them around
Clap them together
Oh, what a sound!

Now lift up one leg
Count "One, two, three"
Now try the other leg
And shake it at me.

Bend at your waist
Reach for the floor
Stand back up straight
Let's do it once more.
  Dick Wilmes

Keep Your Body HEALTHY

Brush your teeth

Eat good food

Exercise

Dress for the weather

Wash your hands

Sleep well

SELF CONCEPT

SNACK

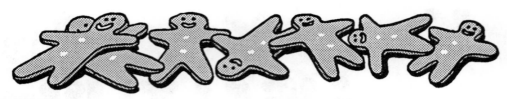

GINGERBREAD CHILDREN

YOU'LL NEED

1 box butterscotch pudding mix
1/2 cup shortening
1/2 cup brown sugar
1 egg
1 1/2 cups flour
1 1/2 t ginger
1/2 t cinnamon
1/2 t baking soda

TO MAKE: Cream the shortening and brown sugar. Add the egg and mix well. Add the pudding, flour, and spices. Mix.

Roll the dough 1/8" to 1/4" thick and cut into one large gingerbread character or lots of small ones. Bake on a greased cookie sheet at 350° for ten minutes.

*from THE EVERYTHING BOOK
by Valerie Indenbaum and Maria Shapiro*

CLASSROOM VISITOR

- Call your local hospital and talk to one of their community service nurses. Set up a time when one of them could come to the center and talk with the children about different things that they can do to stay healthy.

LANGUAGE GAMES

NAME IT

Stand up so that the children can easily see you. Slowly point to different body parts, having the children call out the name of each part as you point. As they understand the game, begin pointing a little faster, faster, faster and then slower, slower. Each time you play change the tempo of the game.

I CAN

Cut a giant can shape from butcher paper. Bring it and a marker to circle time. Tell the children to think of things their bodies can do. As they think of things, call them out and you will write them on the can. To help the children begin to think, say, "When we go outside I see you using your bodies in lots of different ways. I know that you can make them run, so I'm going to write `run' on the can. (Do it.) What else can you do?"

Hang the can at the children's eye level. Add to it as the children think of more activities. Every couple of days, read the list to the children. If you fill one can, cut out another one and continue the activity.

I Can

Run
Build in the sand
Hang on the bars

LANGUAGE GAMES

BODY TALK

Move your body to send a message to the children. After it has spoken, have the children tell you what it said. Here are some starters:
- Wave to say, "*Hi.*"
- Put finger on your lips to say, "*Please be quiet.*"
- Lay your head on your hands to say, "*Time to rest.*"
- Wave your hand towards you to say, "*Come here.*"
- Pinch your nose to say, "*Bad smell.*"
- Point to your eyes to say, "*Look.*"
- Stretch your arm out with your palm at a right angle to say, "*Stop.*"
- Put your hand up to your ear to say, "*Listen.*"
- Lay your hand on your heart to say, "*I love you.*"

MY HANDS HELP ME

Name a body part such as `hands.' Have the children hold up their hands and shake-shake-shake them all around. Now have the children look at their hands and think of the things their hands help them do, such as color or dig. As the children think of things, call them out. Keep thinking!

Name a different body part such as `mouth.' Have the children open and shut their mouths and then think of things that their mouths help them do. Continue with other body parts.

HOW TALL ARE YOU?

Before circle time cut out a 6 to 6½ foot sheet of newsprint or butcher paper. Have an adult lie down on the paper and a second adult draw around her shape to make a giant silhouette.

Tape the adult's shape, with the feet at the floor, on a wall/door near the group area. Have a child come up to the shape. Say to the child, "*Point to one of Ms. Betty's hands.*" (The child does.) Continue, letting children point to other body parts such as the feet, arms, head, hair, neck, and so on.

Now ask a child to stand next to the shape. With your hand, measure where the child comes in relation to the silhouette. Have the child look where your hand is. Write his/her name on the silhouette. Mark several more children's heights, then continue measuring during free choice time. Finish the activity over the next several days.

SELF CONCEPT

ACTIVE GAMES

MOVE IT   Have the children stand in a group. Look at one child and say, *"Amelia, I'm looking at your arm. MOVE IT!"* The child moves her arm how ever she wishes. The others follow her action. After awhile name another child and continue the game following that child's movement.

HOKEY POKEY   Get the *`Hokey-Pokey'* song or simply sing it as you play. Have the children form a circle and begin moving to the directions of the song.

JACK BE NIMBLE JUMP   Have a candle (real, paper towel or toilet paper roll) for each of the children. Have them hold their candles up and say the *`JACK BE NIMBLE'* rhyme. Then have them put their candles on the floor. Repeat the rhyme. When they say the line, *"Jack jump over the candlestick,"* have the children jump over their candles.

JACK BE NIMBLE

Jack be nimble,
Jack be quick,
Jack jump over the candlestick.

Keep the candles on the floor, have the children repeat the rhyme doing other tricks with their candles.
- *"Jack, walk around your candlestick."*
- *"Jack, hop over your candlestick."*
- *"Jack, hold your candlestick way up high."*
- *"Jack, gently put your toes on your candlestick."*
- *"Jack, march around your candlestick."*
- Last one. *"Jack, put your candlestick in the basket."*

ACTIVE GAMES

FINGER EXERCISES

Have the children hold up their fingers and exercise as you give the directions:

- Bend your fingers up and down - up and down - up and down. Chant "*Up and down*" as you move. Relax and then continue.
- Streeeeeeetch your fingers as tall as you can. Relax and streeeetch again.
- Close your fingers into a tight fist. Relax. Repeat.
- Dance your fingers all around as fast as you can - as slowly as you can. Relax.
- Spread your fingers as far apart as you can - close them up again. Relax. Repeat several times.
- Touch the tips of your fingers together and swim like fish. Hum as you swim.
- Touch the tips of your fingers together and press real hard. Relax. Press again and relax. Do several more times.

BOOKS

MARC BROWN — *ARTHUR'S TOOTH*
BARBARA BRENNER — *BODIES*
JEAN HOLZENTHALER — *MY FEET DO*
JEAN HOLZENTHALER — *MY HANDS CAN*
BILL MARTIN — *HERE ARE MY HANDS*
DR. SEUSS — *THE FOOT BOOK*

SELF CONCEPT

CLOTHING

FOR OPENERS

BRING A BIG CUDDLY TEDDY BEAR OR OTHER STUFFED ANIMAL TO SHOW THE CHILDREN. TELL THEM THAT 'TEDDY' ENJOYS DOING LOTS OF DIFFERENT ACTIVITIES, BUT HE ALWAYS HAS TROUBLE KNOWING WHAT TO WEAR. 'TEDDY' WAS WONDERING IF THEY WOULD HELP HIM.

CREATE A VARIETY OF SITUATIONS IN WHICH 'TEDDY' WOULD NEED TO WEAR DIFFERENT CLOTHES AND LET THE CHILDREN TALK ABOUT WHAT WOULD BE APPROPRIATE. FOR EXAMPLE:

● "TEDDY IS GOING TO WALK DOWN HIS DRIVEWAY TO GET THE MAIL. HE LOOKS OUTSIDE AND SEES THAT IT IS RAINING. WHAT SHOULD TEDDY WEAR TO THE MAILBOX?" (TALK ABOUT IT.)

● "TEDDY AND HIS DAD ARE GOING TO THE GROCERY STORE. TEDDY'S DAD REMINDS HIM THAT IT IS COLD OUTSIDE. WHAT SHOULD TEDDY WEAR TO THE GROCERY STORE?" (TALK ABOUT IT.)

● "TEDDY AND A BUNCH OF HIS FRIENDS ARE GOING SWIMMING AT THE BEACH. HE KNOWS THAT HE SHOULD BRING HIS PAIL AND SHOVEL TO PLAY WITH ON THE SAND, BUT WHAT CLOTHES DOES HE NEED?" (TALK ABOUT IT.)

FINGERPLAYS

RAINY DAY FUN

Slip on your raincoat,
Pull on galoshes,
Wading in puddles
Makes splishes and sploshes.

I AM A COBBLER

I am a cobbler
And this is what I do:
Rap - tap - a - tap
To mend my shoe.

WHAT ARE YOU WEARING ?

TEACHER:
Blue, blue, blue, blue
Who is wearing blue today?
Blue, blue, blue, blue,
Who is wearing blue?

CHILDREN: (Those wearing blue
            stand up and say):

I am wearing blue today.
Look at me and you will say,
"Blue, blue, blue, blue,
You are wearing blue today."

ALL BY MYSELF
(Use for riddles.)

Hat on head, chin strap here,
Snap just so, you see.
I can put my _____ on
All by myself — just me.

One arm in, two arms in,
Buttons one, two, three.
I can put my _____ on
All by myself — just me.

Toes in first, heels push down,
Pull, pull, pull and whee!
I can put my _____ on
All by myself — just me.

Fingers here, thumbs right here,
Hands are warm as can be.
I can put my _____ on
All by myself — just me.

SNACK

BREAD PEOPLE

YOU'LL NEED

Bread
Spreadable cheese/peanut butter
Vegetables
Fruits
Raisins
People cookie cutters

TO MAKE: Soften the cheeses. Cut the fruits and vegetables into small pieces/slices. Cut each slice of bread into a `person.'
   Let children spread the `bread people' with cheese or peanut butter, and then dress them with fruits and vegetables.

FIELD TRIPS

- Take a walk around your neighborhood and look for other people who are outside such as the letter carrier, construction workers, adults taking babies for walks, truck drivers, and so on. Talk about the clothes these people have on and why they might be wearing them.

17

LANGUAGE GAMES

LOOK CAREFULLY
Bring several large pictures of people to circle time. (Clothing catalogues are good resources.) Hold up one of them. Tell the children to look at it carefully and name the different clothes which the person is wearing. As they are naming the clothes, encourage them to look carefully and find, even those clothes which are hard to see, such as socks tucked between shoes and pants. Repeat with another picture.
VARIATION:
Glue each picture to a large sheet of construction paper. As the children name each piece of clothing, write it on the paper. When you're finished with each picture, read the words to the children. Hang the mini-posters at the children's eye level.

WHAT'S IN THE CLOSET ?
Tell the children to cover their eyes and think of the clothes in their closets. Open their eyes. Show them a hanger. Have a roll of shelf paper and a marker. Say, *"What clothes do you have in your closet that are hanging on hangers?"* Write down what they say.
After naming the clothes on hangers, cut the shelf paper and clip it to the hanger with clothespins. Hang the list at their eye level and add to it as children think of more clothes hanging on hangers.
Now show the children a hook. Talk about clothes in their closets which are hanging from hooks. After naming all of those, talk about clothes which are on shelves, on the floor, in boxes, bags, and so on.

CLOTHING SORT
Collect a variety of clothes worn by different family members - baby, child, teenager, mom, dad. Put them in a bag and bring them to circle time. Pull out the clothes one at a time. Have the children tell you what it is and who would wear it. Make piles for each family member. Continue until all of the clothes have been sorted according to who would wear them.

LANGUAGE GAMES

WHERE ARE YOU GOING?

Put different types of footwear into a box. Bring the box to circle time.

Tell the children to stick out their shoes. Talk about the types of shoes they are wearing and the fact that they are good for school. Show the children the box. Tell them that you have brought different pairs of footwear for them to look at. Hold up one pair. Ask the children who might wear these shoes, where s/he could be going, and why the person might have chosen that pair to wear. Continue with other pairs.

EXTENSION:
Display the footwear for the children look at, talk about, and even try on.

GETTING DRESSED

Tell the children to pretend that they are just getting out of bed. Let them stretch and yawn and then go into the bathroom to brush their teeth, wash, and comb their hair. Now back in the bedroom, they should get dressed. First put on their underwear. Ask the children what they put on next. (Put it on.) What's next. (Do it.) Continue talking with the children and putting on their clothes until they are ready for breakfast.

Breakfast is over and it's time for school. What other clothes might they need to put on? Put them on and sing this simple song.

OFF TO SCHOOL
(tune: Mary Had A Little Lamb)

Now we're going off to school,
Off to school, off to school.
Now we're going off to school,
To sing and dance and play.
  Liz Wilmes

19

ACTIVE GAMES

PASS THE MITTEN   Put pairs of mittens in a box and bring them to circle time. Put a record on the record player. Hand one mitten to a child. Start the music. As the music is playing have the children pass the mitten. Stop the music. The child with the mitten should hold it up and tell what color/s it is, and then put it behind his back. Give a mitten to another child, start the music and play again. Continue in this manner until all of the mittens have been passed. Now have the children put the mittens in front of them. One at a time pair the mittens and put them back into the box.

USE YOUR EYES   Have your children use their hands for binoculars as they say the `USE YOUR EYES' rhyme. Once they know it, name a different piece of clothing in the third line and a different action in the fourth line. Have those children who are wearing the clothing you named do the action.

USE YOUR EYES

Use your eyes, use your eyes,
You can look and see,
If you're wearing brown shoes,
Hop, hop, hop to me.

BOOKS

JOAN BLOS — *MARTIN'S HATS*
DON FREEMAN — *POCKET FOR CORDUROY*
STEVEN KELLOGG — *THE MYSTERY OF THE MISSING RED MITTEN*
EVE RICE — *NEW BLUE SHOES*
ESPHYR SLOBODKINA — *CAPS FOR SALE*

FIVE SENSES

FOR OPENERS

MAKE A `TOUCH AND FEEL BOX' BEFORE CIRCLE TIME. PUT AN OBJECT IN THE BOX. (ORANGE, RAISIN, CARROT)

SHOW THE BOX TO THE CHILDREN. TELL THEM THAT THERE IS SOMETHING IN THE BOX AND THAT YOU WANT THEM TO USE THEIR SENSES TO GUESS WHAT IT MIGHT BE. GIVE THE BOX TO A CHILD AND ASK HIM TO REACH THROUGH THE HOLE, TOUCH THE OBJECT, AND TELL THE OTHERS HOW IT FEELS. THAT CHILD SHOULD PASS THE BOX TO ANOTHER CHILD. HELP THAT CHILD HOLD THE BOX UP TO HIS NOSE. DOES THE OBJECT SMELL? WHAT DOES IT SMELL LIKE? PASS THE BOX TO A THIRD CHILD. HAVE HIM ROLL THE OBJECT AROUND OR SHAKE THE BOX. WHAT DOES THE OBJECT SOUND LIKE? HOW DOES THE OBJECT MOVE? LET THE CHILD PASS IT TO A FOURTH FRIEND. THAT CHILD SHOULD PEAK THROUGH THE OPENING AND TELL THE OTHERS WHAT THE OBJECT LOOKS LIKE, FOR EXAMPLE WHAT COLOR IT IS, SHAPE, ETC. IF THE OBJECT IS EATABLE, HAVE A PIECE OF IT READY FOR THE FIFTH CHILD TO TASTE. HAVE THAT CHILD COVER HIS EYES AND PUT THE SAMPLE INTO HIS MOUTH. HOW DOES IT TASTE?

NOW THAT THE CHILDREN HAVE ALL OF THE CLUES, LET THEM GUESS WHAT THE OBJECT MIGHT BE. SLOWLY OPEN THE BOX AND TAKE IT OUT, SO THAT ALL OF THE CHILDREN CAN SEE WHAT IT IS. IF IT IS A FOOD, HAVE IT FOR SNACK.

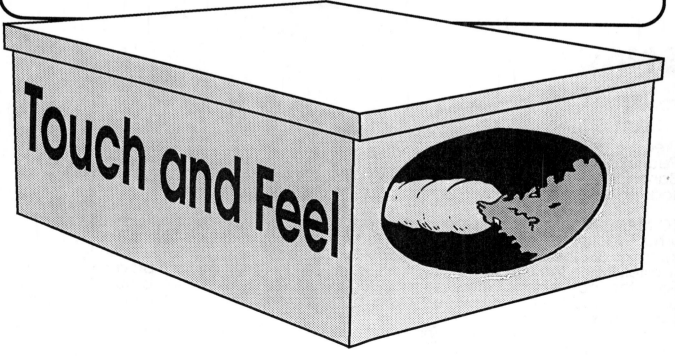

SELF CONCEPT

21

FINGERPLAYS

FIVE SENSES

I have five fingers on each hand.
Ten toes on my two feet.
Two ears, two eyes, one nose, one mouth.
With which to gently speak.
My hands can clap.
My feet can tap.
My eyes can quickly see.
My ears can hear.
My nose can smell.
My mouth can speak this rhyme.

OCEAN SHELL

I found a great big shell one day,
Upon the ocean floor.
I held it close up to my ear,
I heard the ocean roar!
I found a tiny little shell one day,
Upon the ocean sand.
The waves had worn it nice and smooth,
It felt nice in my hand.

EYES TO SEE WITH

Eyes to see with,
Ears to hear with,
Nose to smell with,
Tongue to taste with.
Feet to run with,
Hands to touch with,
I'm a lucky child
Aren't you?

SHHHHHH!

Shhhh —- be very quiet.
Shhhh —- be very still.
Rest your sleepy, sleepy head.
Close your sleepy, sleepy eyes.
Shhhh —- be very still.
 (What do you hear?)

SOFT KITTY

Soft kitty, warm kitty,
Little ball of fur.
Lazy kitty, pretty kitty,
"Purr, purr, purr."

SNACK

TOAST
YOU'LL NEED

Bread
Peanut butter
Bananas
Toaster (several if you have a large group)

TO MAKE: Bring out the toaster and bread. Hold up one piece of bread. Talk about what it looks like. Put the bread in the toaster and pop it down. After a couple of seconds ask the children to smell the bread. It is toasting. Tell them to listen to the toaster. When the bread is ready, the toaster will go 'bing' and the bread will pop up! Soon the toast is done. Show the toast to the children. How has the bread changed? Break the toast into small pieces. Pass it out to the children. Have the children feel the toast and then taste it.

 At snack make toast again. This time let the children spread their toast with peanut butter and top it with banana slices.

CLASSROOM VISITOR

- Call the department of your local hospital which has charge of vision and hearing screenings for the schools. Make an appointment for one of the nurses to come and check your children's eyes and ears.

LANGUAGE GAMES

IMAGINATION STRETCHERS

Have a very soft stuffed animal. Pass it around for everyone to feel. As the children are touching it, say to them in a whisper voice, *"Think soft — very soft. What do you know that feels like this?"*

- Have a paper plate and a marker. Say to the children, *"Here's a paper plate. Let's fill it with foods we like to taste."* Write down what they name and hang it in the housekeeping area.

- Put the children in different situations and ask them what they might smell.
"We're in our kitchen, what would we smell?"
"We're at the movie, what would we smell?"

- Have the children think of different sounds in their environment and then make the appropriate sound.
"I hear birds. What sound am I hearing?"
"I hear the fire engine. How does it sound?"
"I hear a car horn. How does it sound?"
"I hear a baby crying. How does she sound?"

- Tell the children to close their eyes and imagine something. Now open their eyes. Have them share what they imagined.

WHAT AM I EATING?

Get several small, easy to eat foods (raisins, pretzels, pieces of apple, bite-size shredded wheats, pieces of pickles). Tell the children to close their eyes and hold out their hands. Pick one food and quickly go to each child, put a piece of food in his hand, and close it up. Have the children put the food in their mouths and chew it up. Talk about what they thought they had eaten. Tell them what it was.

Have them swish their tongues around their mouths to get ready for another food. As before, pass out, eat, and talk about the food. Continue tasting several more foods.

LANGUAGE GAMES

LOOK CAREFULLY

Make a simple eye chart. Let the children pretend that they are getting an eye exam. You be the doctor. Show the children how to make an `E' with their fingers. Hold up the chart. Point to each symbol and have the children move their fingers in the right direction.

FEEL IT

Use the `Touch and Feel Box' which you made for the opening activity. Find several objects which are hard, furry, rough, squishy, and prickly. Set one of each type of object on the floor for everyone to see. Put the rest of the objects in the box.

Talk about each object on the floor. Pass them around for the children to feel. Put them back on the floor. Now give the `Touch and Feel Box' to a child. Ask him to pick up one of the objects in the box, feel it, and decide which object on the floor it is the most like. Take it out of the box and put it with the object on the floor. Pass the box to a second child and let him repeat the activity with another object. Continue. After all of the objects have been sorted, talk about each category.

CLAP LOUDLY, CLAP SOFTLY

Clap a loud-soft rhythm, such as loud-loud-soft-soft. Have the children clap it back. Do several more; then have a child clap a rhythm and everyone clap it back. Continue clapping different rhythms which you and the children have created.

24

ACTIVE GAMES

I SPY Have the children sit in a group. When you give the signal, they should begin to slowly crawl around the room spying for objects on the floor. After several seconds say, "Freeze." The children stop. Ask the children to carefully search the spot they are in. Talk about things which the children see, such as paper, yarn, truck, paper clip, etc. Give the signal again and the children can begin to crawl and spy for more objects. Repeat several more times.

MARCHING BAND Collect paper towel rolls so that each child can have two. Pass out the rolls and show the children how to gently tap them together for rhythm sticks.
   Now warm up the band by having the children march in place while they beat a rhythm with their sticks. Ready for the parade? You lead the band out the door, around the school, and back.

BOOKS

ALIKI — *MY FIVE SENSES*
TANA HOBAN — *LOOK AGAIN*
BILL MARTIN — *BROWN BEAR, BROWN BEAR WHAT DO YOU SEE?*
BILL MARTIN — *POLAR BEAR, POLAR BEAR WHAT DO YOU HEAR?*

SELF CONCEPT

SAFETY

FOR OPENERS

MAKE FINGER PUPPETS FOR EACH OF THE SAFETY OCCUPATIONS AND BRING THEM TO CIRCLE TIME. PUT ONE OF THE PUPPETS ON YOUR FINGERS AND INTRODUCE HIM/HER TO THE CHILDREN. "GOOD MORNING, CHILDREN. I'M SALLY SAWYER, A LIFE GUARD AT THE SWIMMING POOL. THIS MORNING I'D LIKE TO TALK WITH YOU ABOUT SAFETY WHEN YOU ARE AROUND WATER." (TALK WITH THE CHILDREN ABOUT WATER SAFETY — AT THE BEACH, PARK POOL, WADING POOL, BATH TUB.) CONTINUE THE DISCUSSION USING THE OTHER PUPPETS. EXTENSION: PUT THE PUPPETS IN THE LANGUAGE CENTER FOR THE CHILDREN TO USE DURING FREE CHOICE.

FINGERPLAYS

STOP, DROP, AND ROLL

Clothes on fire,
Don't get scared.
STOP!
DROP!
And ROLL!
  Dick Wilmes

GOOD NIGHT

The little candle burns so bright,
It lights a corner of the night.
The flame is hot I'm sure you know.
To turn it off you simply blow.
Wh-h-h-h Good Night!
  Dick Wilmes

SNACK

STOP AND GO LIGHTS

YOU'LL NEED

2 cups apple juice
4 cups water
6 envelopes of plain gelatin
6 oz unsweetened red raspberry gelatin (stop lights)
6 oz unsweetened lime gelatin (go lights)

TO MAKE: In a large bowl, mix one flavor and 3 envelopes of plain gelatin. Pour 1 cup of apple juice and 2 cups of water into a pan and bring it to a boil. Slowly pour the boiling water into the mixing bowl. Stir the water and gelatin together until the gelatin is thoroughly dissolved. Pour the mixture into a 9"x12" pan and put it in the refrigerator to harden. It takes about 3 hours.

   Repeat the recipe using the second gelatin flavor. When both flavors have hardened, take them out of the refrigerator, and let the children cut them into stop and go lights with small round cookie cutters. Put them on a plate for snack. Talk about street safety as you eat.

CLASSROOM VISITOR

- Ask the director of your school to visit your classroom and talk with the children about safety in the halls, outside the school, and so on.

LANGUAGE GAMES

TALK ABOUT

Tell the children about a time when you forgot a safety rule and who helped you remember it. For example, "*I was walking down the street with a friend. We came to the corner. I started to cross the street without looking at the light. My friend grabbed my arm to stop me. She pointed at the light — it was red. I backed up. We waited until the light changed to green; then we looked both ways and crossed the street.*"

   Let the children tell stories about people who have helped them be safe such as their moms/dads. Can they remember times when an adult has said, "*Now, be careful*" or "*STOP*" or "*Wait for me.*" Encourage the children to tell what was happening.

LANGUAGE GAMES

SAFETY RIDDLES Tell the children different riddles naming safety equipment. Here are some starters:

- *"I drive on the street. I have a loud siren. When people need help with a fire, I race to help them. What am I?"*

- *"I am in most cars. Before the driver begins to go, all of the people put me on. An adult helps the baby put hers on. I stop you from bouncing around. What am I?"*

- *"I live on ceilings. I am quiet unless I sense a fire; then I `screeeeeech' as loudly as I can, to alert people to get outside. What am I?"*

- *"People wear me around their chest or waist while swimming. I help you float. What am I?"*

COVER UP Gather five or six pieces of safety equipment such as a fire extinguisher, life vest, horn, smoke detector, cap for electrical outlets, safety strips for the bath tub, and so on. Line them up. Talk about each one.

Now have the children cover their eyes. Cover one object with a paper bag. Have the children uncover their eyes, look at the objects, and figure out which one is covered up. After talking, uncover it, and see if you were correct. Repeat several times.

DIAL 911 FOR SAFETY Show the children how to use their index and small fingers to make a pretend telephone. Have the children practice making emergency phone calls. To do this have a child make his phone and dial `911' or your town's emergency number. You make your phone and answer as if you were the emergency operator. Help the child tell you his situation and where he is. You tell him what to do, and that you are sending emergency help. Repeat this activity with several children each day.

SELF CONCEPT

29

ACTIVE GAMES

SAFETY WALK   Make a `Stop 'N Go Light` by cutting out green and red circles and gluing them to opposite sides of a paint stir stick.

Bring the `Stop 'N Go Light` with you on a walk around the neighborhood. At every crosswalk, parking lot, and driveway, hold up the `STOP` side of your light. Say the `STOP, LOOK, AND LISTEN` rhyme. Turn the light to the `GO` side and safely cross to the other side.

STOP, LOOK, AND LISTEN

Stop, look, and listen
Before you cross the street.
Use your eyes and ears,
Then use your feet.

STOP, DROP, AND ROLL   Have the children sit in a group with an open space in the middle. Set up situations in which children's clothes catch on fire. For example, *"Sarah, you and your brother were playing with matches. Your skirt caught on fire. What should you do?"* All of the children say, *"Stop, drop, and roll."* As the children are giving the directions, Sarah should do the action. Then talk about how unsafe it is to play with matches. Continue with other examples. (at a campfire, playing with a lighter, house on fire, burning candle fell on you, etc.)

BOOKS

DOROTHY CLAD — *SAFETY TOWN SERIES* (10 titles)
LEONARD KESSLER — *TALE OF TWO BICYCLES: SAFETY ON YOUR BIKE*
VIRGINIA POULET — *BLUE BUG'S SAFETY BOOK*
JUDITH VIORST — *TRY IT AGAIN, SAM*

MY FEELINGS

FOR OPENERS

BEFORE CIRCLE TIME MAKE A `FEELINGS WHEEL.'

SHOW THE `FEELINGS WHEEL' TO THE CHILDREN. POINT TO EACH FACE AND TALK ABOUT HOW THAT PERSON MIGHT BE FEELING. PUT THE WHEEL ON THE FLOOR SO THAT EVERYONE CAN SEE IT. HAVE A CHILD FLICK THE SPINNER AND NAME THE FEELING IT POINTS TO. TALK ABOUT TIMES WHEN THE CHILDREN FELT THAT WAY. HAVE ANOTHER CHILD FLICK THE SPINNER AND TALK ABOUT THE FEELING THAT IT INDICATES. CONTINUE SPINNING AND TALKING.

SELF CONCEPT

FINGERPLAYS

IF

If your fingers wiggle,
Cross them one by one,
Until they hug each other.
It really is quite fun.

SNACK

AGGRESSION BALLS

YOU'LL NEED

8 oz peanut butter
2T honey
1/2 cup non-fat powdered milk

TO MAKE: Put all of the ingredients in a large bowl and begin mixing them together. As soon as they form a large ball, put it on the table and let the children knead it until thoroughly mixed. (As the children are kneading, tell them that this is a good activity to work through emotions.) If necessary add more dry milk. Let the children make lots of bite-size balls out of the mixture.

LANGUAGE GAMES

GO FISHING

Before circle time make a `Go Fish' game. Cut out lots of construction paper fish. Draw feeling faces on them. Slip a metal paper clip onto each fish. Make a fishing rod by tying a piece of yarn to a dowel rod and then tying a magnet to the end of the yarn.

Bring the game to circle time. Lay the fish on the floor. Give the fishing rod to a child. All of the children say, *"Go fishing."* The child catches a fish and tells the others what feeling face is on it. The children then talk about different things that might be happening to the fish to make him feel that way. Continue playing by letting others fish.

LANGUAGE GAMES

BEE HAPPY
On a piece of poster board, draw and then cut out a giant bee shape. Bring it and a marker to circle time.
    Have the children think of things that make them happy. Write what they say on the bee. Hang the `Bee Happy` list on a wall at their eye level. Add to it whenever a child thinks of something else that makes him happy. Take time to read the list to the children every couple of days.
EXTENSION:
    Cut out a sad bee and make a `Bee Sad` list; an angry bee for a `Bee Angry` list, and so on.

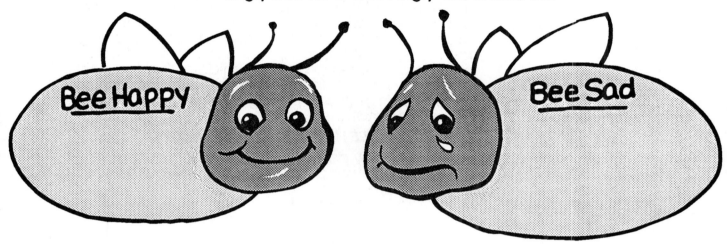

HAPPY OR MAD?
Set up happy and angry situations and tell them to the children. (Without using names, actual classroom situations work well for this activity.) After you have told an incident, each child should decide if he would be happy or mad in that situation. If he would be happy, he should clap his hands together; if he would be mad, he should tap his hands on the floor. Quickly look at the children as they are clapping or tapping. Talk about why they would be happy/angry in each situation.

HOORAY FOR FEELINGS
Say a series of four or five words, one of which is a `feeling` word and the others are not, for example *"tomato, paper, fingers, sad, chair."* When you say the `feeling` word, the children shout, "HOORAY." Continue with other series.

TALK ABOUT
Talk with the children about important people in their lives and what makes these people feel happy, angry, sad, silly, and so on. You could begin the discussion by saying, *"What makes your mom really happy?"* (Talk.) *"How can you tell that she is happy?"* (Talk.) Continue with other feelings and different people, such as sisters, grandparents, brothers, dads, etc.

S E L F   C O N C E P T

ACTIVE GAMES

CHARADES   Have the children sit in a group with space in the middle. Name a child to go into the middle. Tell a short story about an incident in the classroom (no names except the child in the middle). For example, *"Sally, you are painting at the easel and a friend bumps your arm. Show us how you would feel."* The others call out what feeling they think the child is portraying. Talk about the incident and the feeling.

IF YOU'RE HAPPY   Make pairs of large construction paper hearts showing different feelings — happy, angry, sad, etc.
    Have the children stand in a circle and hold hands. Mix up the hearts and lay them face up in the middle. Have the children walk in a circle and sing the first verse of the song. When they've finished have two children go into the middle, find the pair of `happy hearts' and set them next to each other. Continue singing and pairing until all of the hearts have been matched.

IF YOU'RE HAPPY AND YOU KNOW IT

If you're happy and you know it, clap your hands.
If you're happy and you know it, clap your hands.
If you're happy and you know it,
Then your face will really show it.
If you're happy and you know it, clap your hands.

If you're angry and you know it, pound your fist.

If you're sad and you know it, wipe your eyes.

If you're scared and you know it, shake all over.

If you're sleepy and you know it, stretch your arms.

BOOKS

ALIKI — *FEELINGS*
MAJORIE FLACK — *ASK MR. BEAR*
MERCER MAYER — *THERE'S A NIGHTMARE IN MY CLOSET*
JOANNE BRISSON MURPHY — *FEELINGS*
JUDITH VIORST — *ALEXANDER AND THE TERRIBLE, HORRIBLE, NO GOOD,*
        VERY BAD DAY.
CHARLOTTE ZOLOTOW — *WILLIAM'S DOLL*

FAMILIES

TALK WITH THE CHILDREN ABOUT ACTIVITIES WHICH DIFFERENT FAMILY MEMBERS DO IN THE MORNING. START BY ASKING YOUR CHILDREN TO NAME THINGS THEY DO. PICK ANOTHER FAMILY MEMBER, MAYBE A BROTHER. FIRST ASK WHO HAS A BROTHER. NAME THINGS HE DOES IN THE MORNING. CONTINUE WITH THE OTHER FAMILY MEMBERS.

ON ANOTHER DAY REPEAT THE ACTIVITY TALKING ABOUT ACTIVITIES WHICH THE FAMILY MEMBERS DO AT NIGHT.

CUT OUT A GIANT SUN SHAPE FROM YELLOW POSTER BOARD AND ON A THIRD DAY BRING IT AND A MARKER TO CIRCLE TIME. MAKE A LIST OF DIFFERENT ACTIVITIES WHICH FAMILIES DO IN THE MORNING BY LETTING THE CHILDREN REPEAT AND ADD TO ACTIVITIES THEY ORIGINALLY THOUGHT OF. WRITE THEM ON THE SUN. USE BOTH SIDES IF NECESSARY. HANG THE SUN LOW FROM THE CEILING. REPEAT THIS ACTIVITY WITH A GIANT MOON. HANG IT FROM THE CEILING. TAKE OPPORTUNITIES TO READ THE LISTS TO YOUR CHILDREN.

FINGERPLAYS

HELPING MY DAD

I like to help my dad a lot
To rake the lawn or dry a pot.
It doesn't matter what's to be done.
When we do it together,
It's always more fun!!
  Dick Wilmes

BABY'S NAP

This is a baby ready for a nap.
Lay her down in her mother's lap,
Cover her up so she won't peep.
Rock her 'til she's fast asleep.

MUSIC IN OUR HOME

Mother plays the violin.
Daddy plays the flute.
Big brother blows the horn,
Toot-toot-toot-toot.
Little sister keeps the beat
By clanging on a pot.
And I try to sing along
Whether I know the words or not.

SELF CONCEPT

35

SNACK

FAMILY PIZZAS

YOU'LL NEED

English muffins
Pizza sauce
Sliced mushrooms
Shredded cheese
Pitted ripe olives (optional)

TO MAKE: Spread pizza sauce on the english muffins, add mushrooms, and sprinkle with cheese. Top the pizzas with slices of ripe olives. Toast the pizzas under the broiler until the cheese has melted.

LANGUAGE GAMES

FELT BOARD FUN

Think about the different people who live in your children's families. Cut out magazine pictures representing each type. Back each picture with a piece of felt or magnet tape.

Put the pictures at the top of your felt/magnet board. Point to each family member and talk about who it is. Using some of the members, create a family group in the middle of the board. Let the children name the members of this family. Ask them if any of their families look like this one. Put the members back. Let a child come up and create the next family. Talk about this family. Does anyone's family look like this? Continue, mixing different family groups.

WHO WEARS THESE SHOES?

Get a variety of shoes, boots, slippers, and other footwear which different family members might wear. Set them in an open area so that the children can easily see them. Talk about each pair. Let the children decide which family member would wear it. How can they tell?

LANGUAGE GAMES

FAMILY PETS

Have the children sit in a circle with room in the middle. Be quiet and have the children think about their family pets or pets they wish they had. Call on one child to go into the middle and act like his pet.

The other children watch. After the child stops, the others guess what his pet is. The child then tells them whether his pet is real or pretend. Continue, letting other children share their pets with the class.

OLD MOTHER HUBBARD

Have a large box representing Old Mother Hubbard's cupboard. Set it on the floor with the doors closed. Say the `OLD MOTHER HUBBARD` rhyme. As you say, "*the cupboard was bare*" open the doors and let the children look inside.

Say something like, "*Oh, no. There is no food for the dog. We better go to the grocery store and get him something. What food would he like?*" (Children name foods for the dog.) Continue the discussion, "*Oh no. There is no food for the family either and we have to have dinner. What foods should we buy for ourselves?*" (Children name foods for the family dinner.)
EXTENSION:
Write a shopping list as the children name the foods.

FAMILY WORDS

Tell the children to cover their eyes and take a pretend walk to every room in their house. Now uncover their eyes and let children name the rooms. Have the children cover their eyes again. This time they should picture the furniture in their kitchen. Uncover their eyes and name the furniture. Cover their eyes and picture foods that their families like. Uncover their eyes and name the foods. Continue in this manner to share family words about television shows, favorite games, chores, and so on.

ACTIVE GAMES

FAMILY IN THE HOME

Sing `FAMILY IN THE HOME' with the children. As you sing walk in a circle. At the end of each verse, pause and tell the children which family member is next. Continue until the whole family is in the middle.

Once the children know the tune and how to play the game, let them make up their own verses to create different family structures.

FAMILY IN THE HOME
(tune: Farmer In the Dell)

Mommy in the home,
Mommy in the home, (You choose first child.)
Hi-ho the derry-o,
Mommy in the home.

Mommy takes a son,
Mommy takes a son, (Mommy chooses a son)
Hi-ho the derry-o
Mommy takes a son.

Son takes a daddy.

Daddy takes a daughter.

Daughter takes a sister.

Sister takes a gramma.

Gramma takes cat.

The family stands together,
The family stands together,
Hi-ho the derry-o,
The family stands together.

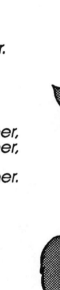

BOOKS

MARC BROWN — *ARTHUR'S BABY*
ANNA G. HINES — *DADDY MAKES THE BEST SPAGHETTI*
RUSSELL HOBAN — *A BABY SISTER FOR FRANCES*
PAT HUTCHINS — *TITCH*
ROBERT KRAUS — *WHOSE MOUSE ARE YOU?*
MERCER MAYER — *ME TOO!*
ANN MORRIS — *LOVING*
JILL MURPHY — *FIVE MINUTES PEACE*
URSEL SCHEFFLER — *A WALK IN THE RAIN*
MARTIN WADDELL — *MY GREAT GRANDPA*

COLORS

FOR OPENERS

CUT DIFFERENT COLORS OF HEAVY YARN ABOUT 12" LONG — ONE
FOR EACH CHILD PLUS SEVERAL MORE. USING A CLOTHESPIN, CLIP ALL
OF THEM TO A HANGER. SHOW THE YARN TO THE CHILDREN.

POINT TO SEVERAL AND NAME THE COLOR. THEN SAY TO A CHILD,
"JOSIE, COME UP AND GET THE `BLACK' PIECE OF YARN." JOSIE
UNCLIPS THE BLACK PIECE AND YOU TIE IT AROUND HER WRIST.
CONTINUE UNTIL ALL OF THE CHILDREN HAVE PIECES OF YARN TIED
AROUND THEIR WRISTS. QUICKLY LET EACH CHILD HOLD UP HIS WRIST
AND NAME THE COLOR OF HIS BRACELET.

EXTENSION: THROUGHOUT THE DAY ENCOURAGE THE CHILDREN TO
LOOK FOR THINGS WHICH MATCH THEIR BRACELETS AND THEN WEAR
THEM HOME AND LOOK FOR MORE.

FINGERPLAYS

USE YOUR EYES

Use your eyes, use your eyes,
You can look and see;
If you have on brown shoes,
Come and stand by me.

FALL LEAVES

Leaf of red, leaf of green,
Prettiest leaf I've ever seen.
Leaf of brown, leaf of gold,
Sometimes flat, sometimes rolled.

Falling from the trees so high,
Blowing in the autumn sky.
Soon the snow will begin to blow,
Then in spring new leaves will grow.
  Dick Wilmes

IN MY EASTER BASKET

Red eggs, yellow eggs,
Green eggs too.
So many colors
I'll share some with you.
  Vohny Moehling

RED LIGHT

Red light says STOP!
Green says GO!
Yellow says CAUTION!
Be sure you know.

BIRTHDAY FIREWORKS

Red, white and blue,
Happy birthday to you.
Fireworks up high,
Lighting the sky.
Happy Birthday to you!
  Vohny Moehling

BASIC CONCEPTS

SNACK

FRUIT KABOBS

YOU'LL NEED

Variety of fruit
Rounded toothpicks
Small paper plates

TO MAKE: Wash/peel and then slice the fruit. Let the children slip several pieces of fruit onto each toothpick and then set them on a large plate. Before passing the kabobs look at the fruit and talk about the different colors.

CLASSROOM VISITOR

- Ask a local artist or an art student from the high school or nearby college to visit your class. Have the artist bring his/her pallet of paints and several brushes with him/her. As s/he is talking with the children have him/her use the classroom easel and paper to show the children how to mix colors and develop new ones.

LANGUAGE GAMES

NAME THAT COLOR

Gather different colored solid scarves and tie them together into one long streamer. Cover the top and bottom of a shoe box. Cut an opening in one end of the box. Put the streamer of scarves in the box.

Hold the box. Tell the children that there is something special inside of it. Ask a child to come up, put his hand in the box, and slowly begin pulling out the surprise. As the child pulls out the streamer of scarves, have the children call out each color. After he has pulled several colors out, switch children and let a second child continue to pull, while the others call out the colors.

When the entire streamer of scarves has been pulled out, let two children hold it at either end. Is it long? Name each color again. Put the scarf back into the box, play again. After you've played several times, see if the children can remember what color scarf comes next, then pull it out. Keep going.

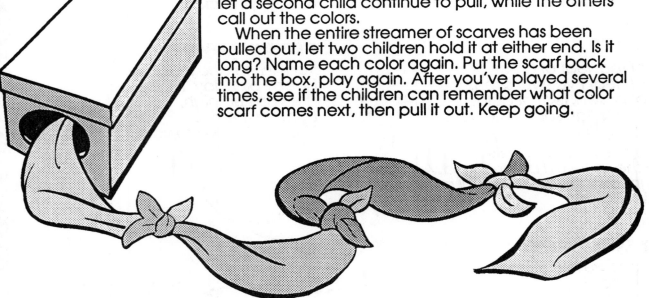

LANGUAGE GAMES

FELT BOARD FUN

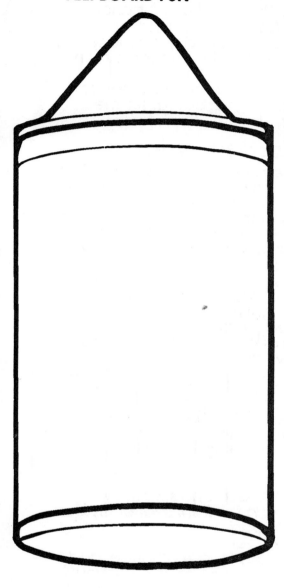

● **All In A Row:** Using the pattern, cut out different colored construction paper/felt crayons. (Put magnet tape on the back of the paper crayons.) Bring the crayons and felt/magnet board to circle time.

Put all of the crayons in a row on the board. Point to each one and have everyone name it. Take the crayons off of the board. Now put three or four crayons in a row back on the board. Point to each one and name it. Have the children cover their eyes. Hold a piece of paper over the sequence. Have them uncover their eyes and name the first color in the sequence. Uncover the first crayon. Was that the color? Continue naming and uncovering the rest of the sequence. Clear the board. Repeat the game using different sequences.

● **Crayon Match:** Make pairs of crayon shapes. Put one of each color on the felt/magnet board. Pass out the matching crayons. Teach your children the rhyme. Say it as they match each pair of crayons.

> **CRAYON MATCH:**
>
> *I'm pointing to a crayon,*
> *Who has the twin?*
> *Bring it up right now*
> *And you will surely grin!* (Everyone cheer.)
> Liz Wilmes

COLOR TRIPS

Say to the children, "*Today we're going to take a trip to the grocery store. We are only going to buy things that are 'white.' What are we going to put in our grocery cart?*" (Here are some starters: eggs, milk, cottage cheese, crackers, ice cream) Say another color and have the children name things that they would put in their grocery cart that are that color. Continue with more colors.

On other days take different trips — such as to the zoo, "*What color animals will you see?*" To the park, "*What things are green?*" To the beach, "*What color bathing suits do you see and who is wearing each one?*"

BASIC CONCEPTS

LANGUAGE GAMES

**GERI GIRAFFE
FINDS HER
COLORS**

Before circle time make a large Geri Giraffe out of yellow construction paper. Put a piece of magnet stripping on her backside. Cut out 8-10 different colors of construction paper spots and put a piece of magnet stripping on each one. Put the spots in an envelope.

Bring Geri, a magnet board, and the envelope to circle time. Put Geri on the magnet board. Tell the children this story.

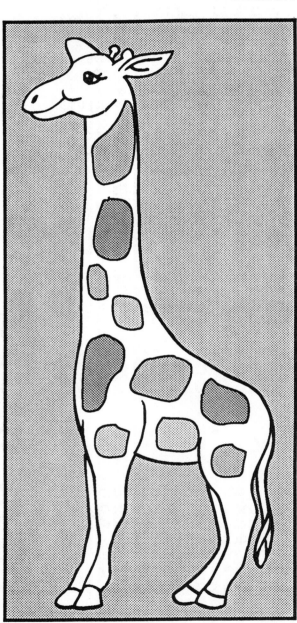

GERI GIRAFFE FINDS HER SPOTS

"Yesterday when I was leaving school, Geri stopped me. She was very upset, for she had lost all of her spots. I told her that I had not seen them, but that I would look for them. I looked for awhile, but couldn't find them. I told Geri I would continue looking tomorrow; then, I turned out the lights and went home. The next day I woke up from a good night sleep. I stretched and yawned. (Let the children do it.) *I got ready to come to school. I opened the front door and went to my car. I got in and was buckling my seat belt when I saw this envelope next to me.* (Hold up the envelope.) *I was so surprised. On the front it said, "Give this to Geri." At first I couldn't imagine what it might be, then I remembered what Geri had said to me before I had left school.* (Talk with the children about what might be in the envelope.)

I rushed into school with the envelope. I walked right up to Geri and said to her, "Look what was on the front seat of my car! It is an envelope addressed to you. Can I open it for you?" Geri said, "Yes, yes!" I opened the envelope, looked inside, and said to Geri, "You'll be so happy, but you'll also be very surprised!" (Open the envelope and slowly pull out one spot. Ask the children what color the spot is. Put it on Geri. Continue pulling out the spots, naming the colors, and adding each one to Geri. After Geri has all of her spots back, ask her,) *"Well Geri what do you think of your new spots?" She was so excited, that all she could say was, "Thank you, I love my new colors. I'll look so bright when I walk around!"*

43

ACTIVE GAMES

BUZZ AROUND THE GARDEN

Before circle time make 7-8 different colored construction paper flowers.

Have the children sit in a circle with their hands behind their backs. Pick one child to be the bee in the garden, and sit in the middle with his eyes covered. Quietly put one flower in a child's hand. Everyone say to the bee, "Bee in the garden, fly around until you find a `red' flower to land on." The bee uncovers his eyes and begins flying around. All of the other children quietly start buzzing. As the bee gets closer to the `red' flower, the children should buzz louder and louder. If the bee starts flying away from the flower they should buzz more quietly. Taking signals from the loudness of the buzzing, the bee should find and land on the `red' flower and then give it to you.

Choose another bee to go into the middle and play again. Continue until the bees have landed on all of the flowers.

ACTIVE GAMES

RED LIGHT, GREEN LIGHT

Make a simple `stop and go' light by cutting out a 6" red and a 6" green construction paper circle and gluing them back-to-back on a paint stir stick.

Tell the children an exercise. Hold up the green light to begin moving. Keep exercising until you flash the red light to stop. Tell them the new exercise, and then flash green for them to begin. Continue using the red and green light to signal when to stop and start exercising.

IF YOU'RE WEARING RED

Have the children sit in a group. Say the rhyme using a different color each time, and have the children take their bows.

IF YOU'RE WEARING RED

If you're wearing red today,
If you're wearing red,
Stand up now
And take your bow
And sit right down again.
  Liz Wilmes

BOOKS

TANA HOBAN — *IS IT RED? IS IT YELLOW? IS IT BLUE?*
CROCKETT JOHNSON — *HAROLD AND THE PURPLE CRAYON*
ANN JONAS — *COLOR DANCE*
BILL MARTIN — *BROWN BEAR, BROWN BEAR, WHAT DO YOU SEE?*
MERLE PEEK — *MARY WORE HER RED DRESS AND
          HENRY WORE HIS GREEN SNEAKERS*
JOHN REISS — *COLORS*
KATHY STINSON — *RED IS BEST*
ELLEN WALSH — *MOUSE PAINT*

ALPHABET

HAVE THE CHILDREN SIT IN A GROUP, COVER THEIR EYES, AND THINK OF PLACES WHERE THEY SEE LETTERS AND WORDS. OPEN THEIR EYES. LET THEM START NAMING ALL OF THE PLACES, SUCH AS THE NEWSPAPER, BOOKS, SIGNS, CEREAL BOOKS, MENUS, —- KEEP GOING. VARIATION: CUT A GIANT `E` OUT OF POSTER BOARD AND BRING IT TO CIRCLE TIME. WRITE DOWN WHERE THE CHILDREN SEE LETTERS. HANG IT FROM THE CEILING LOW ENOUGH TO READ. ADD MORE PLACES AS THE CHILDREN THINK OF THEM. MAYBE YOU'LL USE BOTH SIDES.

newspaper, magazine, book
sign
letter
birthday card
cereal box
menu

SNACK

SOFT PRETZELS

YOU'LL NEED

1 pkg. yeast
1 1/2 cup warm water
1 t salt
1/2 t sugar
4 cups flour
1 egg, beaten
Coarse salt, optional

TO MAKE: Measure the warm water into a large mixing bowl. Sprinkle the yeast over the water and stir until it looks soft. Add the salt, sugar, and flour. Mix and knead the dough. Cover the bowl, set it in a warm place, and let the dough rise until doubled. Punch the dough down and divide it into small pieces. Give every child one to roll and twist into a letter.

Grease the cookie sheets and lay the letters on them. Brush each letter with beaten egg and sprinkle with coarse salt. Bake at 425° for 12-15 minutes.

FIELD TRIP

- Call your local newspaper printer and make an appointment for your class to visit the printing shop and watch the town newspaper being printed.

LANGUAGE GAMES

LETTER ECHO　　Cup your hands and say a letter to the children. Have the children cup their hands and echo it back to you. Continue with more letters.

MAGNET BOARD FUN　　Cut 52, 2"x3" pieces of light-colored construction paper. Print the capital and lower case letters on them. Back each one with a piece of magnet stripping. (Easy magnet boards: cookie sheet, kitchen counter-top protector, large automobile oil pan)

- **Name That Letter:** Bring the letters and magnet board to circle time. Put three or four letters on the board. Point to the first one and have the children name it. Continue until all of the letters are on the board. Take them off one at a time, letting the children name them again as you do.

- **Pick Your Letter:** Put the letters in the middle of the circle. Say, "*Who sees a letter they know?*" (Children respond.) Say to a child, "*Sara, pick your letter.*" As she gets it, have her hold it up, name it, and put it on the magnet board.

LANGUAGE GAMES

ALPHABET SOUP Out of black poster board, cut a giant soup pot. Make two sets of alphabet cards. Lay the soup pot on the floor. Pass out one set of alphabet cards to the children. Have them lay their cards on the floor in front of them. You keep the other set.

Hold up your first card and say, "*I'm putting an `A` in the soup pot. Whose coming with me?*" The child with the `A` puts his in too. Continue pairing the letters and adding them to your soup.
EXTENSION: Make real alphabet soup with the children and have it for a snack.

CLAP FOR THE LETTERS Begin saying a series of words. In the series, say a letter. When the children hear a letter name, they should clap. Continue the series and add more letters. For example, "*Apple, pencil, shoe, Z* (children clap), *book, table, H* (children clap), *paper, cup, cookie, rug, sandwich, M* (children clap), and so on.

NAME A LETTER Have the children stand as they come to circle time, call out a letter, and then sit down. When everyone has come, sing the *ALPHABET SONG* together.

ACTIVE GAMES

PASS ONE LETTER

Have the children sit in a circle. Teach them the song PASS ONE LETTER. Hand a child letter card. Start singing the song and passing the letter. Whoever has the letter at the end of the song should hold it up for everyone to see. Call out what it is. Give a second child another letter. Begin singing and passing two letters. At the end, name both letters. Continue adding letters until it becomes too many to pass. Start over with one letter.

PASS ONE LETTER
(tune: HERE WE GO 'ROUND THE MULBERY BUSH?)

Pass one letter 'round and 'round
'Round and 'round; 'round and 'round.
Pass one letter 'round and 'round
'Round the circle.

Pass two letters 'round and 'round

Pass three letters 'round and 'round

Continue.

PICK A NAME

Before circle time cut 3"x8" strips of lightweight cardboard, one for each child. Write each child's name on a card.

Have the children stand in a circle holding hands. Put all of the name cards, face up, in the middle of the circle. Begin playing music. Have the children start walking in a circle. Stop the music. Call on a child. That child goes into the middle, picks up his name card, and gives it to you. Continue until everyone has picked his name card.

Set the game up again, only this time encourage the children to pick another person's name card, read it, and give it to you.

BOOKS

TERRY BERGER — *BEN'S ABC DAY*
KATE GREENAWAY — *A-APPLE PIE*
TANA HOBAN — *A,B, SEE*
ARNOLD LOBEL — *ON MARKET STREET*

BASIC CONCEPTS

NUMBERS

FOR OPENERS

USING THE PATTERNS, CUT OUT FELT BOARD NUMERALS. BRING THE NUMERALS AND FELT BOARD TO CIRCLE TIME.

PUT ONE NUMERAL ON THE FELT BOARD. WHISPER IT TO THE CHILDREN. HAVE THEM SHOUT IT BACK TO YOU. TAKE IT OFF OF THE BOARD. PUT UP ANOTHER NUMERAL. SHOUT ITS NAME TO THE CHILDREN. HAVE THEM WHISPER IT BACK. CONTINUE.

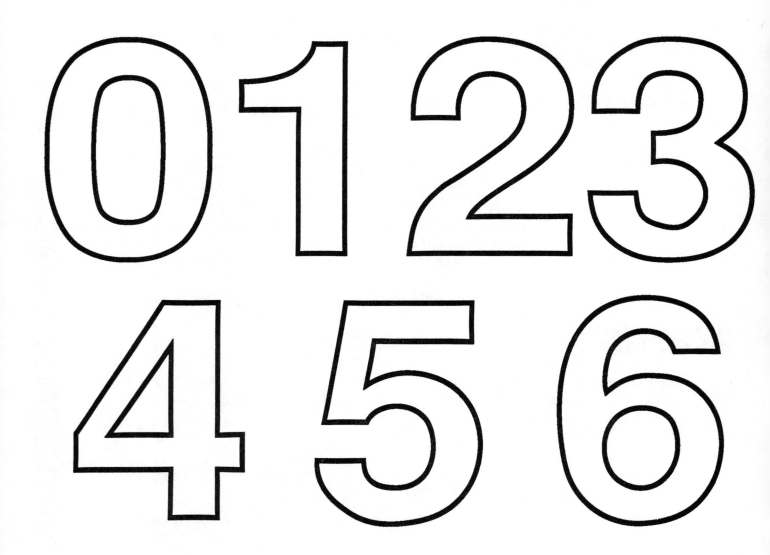

 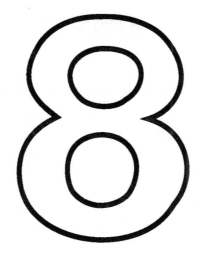 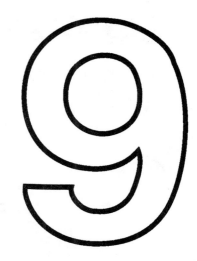

FINGERPLAYS

HOP, HOP, HOP

Find a foot and hop, hop, hop!
When we're tired we stop, stop, stop.
Turn around and count to ten,
Find a foot and hop again!

CLAP YOUR HANDS

Clap your hands 1,2,3.
Clap your hands just like me
Roll your hands 1,2,3.
Roll your hands just like me.

HERE'S A BALL

Here's a ball.
And here's a ball.
A great big ball I see.
Shall we count them?
Are you ready?
1, 2, 3!

THERE'S A BUG

1,2,3 there's a bug on me.
Where did he go?
I don't know.

SNACK

ANTS ON A LOG

YOU'LL NEED

Celery
Cream cheese
Raisins

TO MAKE: Wash the celery and cut it into sections. Let the children spread cream cheese onto the celery pieces and then top them with raisins. Have the children count their `ants' as they are putting them on the `logs.'

BASIC CONCEPTS

LANGUAGE GAMES

10·9·8·7·6·5·4·3·2...

COUNT DOWN   Cut out a giant moon shape from yellow poster board. Bring it and a marker to circle time.

Tell the children that they are going to take a trip to the moon, but they can only bring one thing. Think about it. As each child decides what he wants to bring, have him call it out. You write his name and the object on the moon. After everyone has named his object, read the list to the children. Any changes? Punch a hole near the top of the moon and hang it from the ceiling, low enough to easily read.

Now get ready to blast off. (Have the children crouch down.) Starting at ten, count down to one — then *"Blast-Off."* Have the children blast-off and fly to the moon.

COUNT TO TEN   Count to 10 in English with the children. Count to 10 again, this time in Spanish — *uno, dos, tres, cuatro, cinco, seis, siete, ocho, nueve, diez.* Try it again. How about French — *un, deux, trois, quatre, cinq, six, sept, huit, neuf, dix.*

HOW MANY DO I HAVE?   Bring a bucket filled with multiples of five/six different objects, such as 4 pencils, 7 tennis balls, 5 blocks, 9 crayons, 1 book, and so on. Begin taking out one type of object. Have the children count as you take the object out. Lay the objects in a row. After they are all out of the bucket, touch each one and count again. How many? Continue with the other objects.

WHAT'S MISSING   Cut out felt board numerals. Put them in order on your felt board. Point to each numeral and count with the children. Have them cover their eyes. Remove one numeral. Uncover their eyes and call out the missing numeral. Put it back. Point to the numerals and count again. Continue.

NUMBER HUNT   Have the children look around the room for numbers. Tell everyone where they are. Name them. Now use your hands to make binoculars and look around for more numerals. Point them out and name them.

ACTIVE GAMES

WALK AROUND THE NUMBERS

Cut poster board into 12" squares — one for each child. Write a numeral from 1-10 on each one.

Pass out the numerals. Have each child hold his up and the others call out what it is. Have the children set the number cards in front of them, stand up, and hold hands. Start playing music and have the children walk around the number cards. Stop the music. The children should stop by a card. Call on several children to hold up the card in front to them and everyone call out each number. Continue in this manner.

SIMON SAYS

You be Simon and give the children directions using numbers. Count together as the children follow the orders which Simon gives them.

"Simon says, `Hop up and down 3 times.'"
"Simon says, `Slowly clap 6 times.'" "Quickly."
"Simon says, `Twirl your arms 4 times.'"
"Simon says, `Nod your head side to side 10 times.'"

Continue with more directions from Simon.

Last command. *"Simon says, `Sit cross-legged on the floor one time.'"*

BOOKS

MOLLY BANG — *TEN, NINE, EIGHT*
DAVID BENNETT — *ONE COW MOO MOO*
ERIC CARLE — *ROOSTERS OFF TO SEE THE WORLD*
TANA HOBAN — *COUNT AND SEE*
PAT HUTCHINS — *THE DOORBELL RANG*
MERLE PEEK — *ROLL OVER! A COUNTING GAME*
MAURICE SENDAK — *ONE WAS JOHNNY*
JEFF SHEPPARD — *THE RIGHT NUMBER OF ELEPHANTS*
NANCY TAFURI — *HAVE YOU SEEN MY DUCKLING?*
OLIVE WADSWORTH — *OVER THE MEADOW*

SHAPES

BEFORE CIRCLE TIME, MAKE `SALLY AND SAMMY SHAPE' STICK PUPPETS. TO MAKE THE PUPPETS, DRAW THEIR BASIC OUTLINES ON POSTER BOARD, AND THEN DRAW THE SHAPES ON THEIR BODIES. GLUE A PAINT STIR STICK/TONGUE DEPRESSOR TO THEIR BACKSIDES.

INTRODUCE THE PUPPETS TO YOUR CHILDREN. GIVE ONE PUPPET TO ONE CHILD AND THE OTHER PUPPET TO A SECOND CHILD. HAVE THEM LOOK AT THEIR PUPPETS, POINT TO A SHAPE ON EACH ONE, NAME IT, AND THEN HAND THEIR PUPPETS TO TWO OTHER CHILDREN. THESE CHILDREN SHOULD POINT TO AND NAME TWO OTHER SHAPES ON THE PUPPETS. CONTINUE UNTIL THE CHILDREN HAVE NAMED ALL OF SAMMY'S AND SALLY'S SHAPES.

EXTENSION:
OUT OF COLORED POSTER BOARD, MAKE A DUPLICATE SET OF SHAPES FOR EACH PUPPET. PUT EACH SET IN A CONTAINER. LAY SALLY AND/OR SAMMY ON THE TABLE. DRESS THE PUPPET BY MATCHING THE PIECES TO THE OUTLINES ON THEIR SHAPES.

FINGERPLAYS

THE WINDOW

See the window I have here,
So big and high and square;
I can stand in front of it
And see the things out there.

GIFT BOXES

Gift boxes, gift boxes, everywhere.
Empty now, they're lighter than air.
Some tiny as bugs, one big as a bear.
Round, rectangular, even square.
  Vohny Moehling

BASIC CONCEPTS

SNACK

CRACKER COLLECTION

YOU'LL NEED
Wide variety of different shaped crackers

TO MAKE: Have a bowl for each type of cracker. Let the children put the crackers in the bowls. As they do, talk about the different shapes.

At snack time give each child a small plate. Pass the crackers around the table. Let the children help themselves to each type. After all of the crackers have been passed, talk about the collections on their plates and then enjoy snack.

LANGUAGE GAMES

SHAPE SORT
From poster board, cut giant triangle, circle, square, and rectangle shape cards. Have a container filled with objects accenting these shapes, such as a roll of tape, book, kite, etc.

Lay the shape cards on the floor for everyone to see. Hold up one of the objects and name it. Ask the children which shape card you should set the object on? (Do it.) Continue until all of the objects have been sorted by shape.

IMAGINATION STRETCHER
Using one color poster board, cut out a large, medium and small size circle. Hold up the small circle for the children to see. Say, *"I'm holding a small circle. What does it remind you of?"* Talk about all of the different things that the children think of. Repeat with the medium and large circles. On other days use rectangle, triangle, and square shapes to `streeeeeeeetch' the children's imagination.

CLOTHES SEARCH
Have the children look at their clothes and see if they can find shapes in them, such as eyelet circles in their shoes or belts or patterns in their fabric.

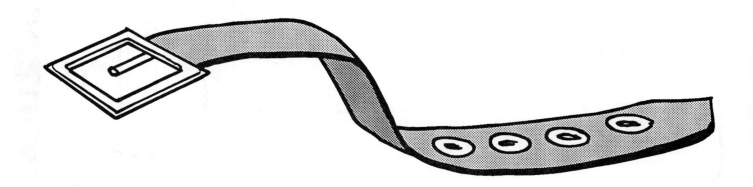

LANGUAGE GAMES

RIDDLE ME A SHAPE
Bring eight to ten objects which accent a shape to circle time. (block, ball, toilet paper roll, ruler, tablet of paper, can, box, hanger, etc.) Set them in a row for everyone to see. Say a riddle about one of them. Let the children guess. If they guess correctly, take it out of the group; if they don't, give them several more clues. Continue with the other objects.

I LOOK FOR
Cut out a large, medium, and small size triangle, circle, square, and rectangle from one color of felt. (If your children know their shapes, make this more challenging by cutting felt shapes in all colors.) Put them in random order on the felt board. Say to the children, *"I am looking for a large circle; when you see one blink your eyes."* (*"Triangle, wiggle your noses; squares, shake your fists; rectangle, point your fingers."*) Have a child come and take it off the felt board and give it to you. Continue until all of the shapes are off of the board.

FEEL THE SHAPES
Cut a large, medium, and small size triangle, circle, square, and rectangle out of fine sandpaper. Glue the shapes to a piece of cardboard. Cut a set of matching shapes out of coarse sandpaper. Put them in a bag.

Bring the board and shapes to circle time. Lay the board on the floor. Have a child come up, pull a shape out of the bag, and hold it up for everyone to see. Everyone names it. The child matches it to the shape on the board.

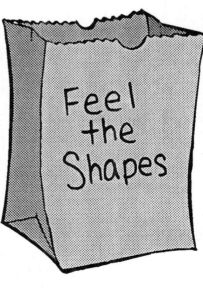

Feel the Shapes

BASIC CONCEPTS

ACTIVE GAMES

HUNT FOR A SHAPE

Cut out lots of construction paper circles, triangles, squares, and rectangles. Before circle time, hide the shapes around the room.

Tell the children that you have hidden shapes for them to find and bring back to you. You will put their names on the shapes and then they can decorate them in the art area. Have the children get ready for the hunt and then say, *"Hunt for a shape."*

FREEZE

Walk to each child, ask him what shape he would like you to draw on his fist, and then using washable marker, draw that shape. Have dancing music ready.

Say to the children, *"When I start the music, everyone begin dancing. When I stop the music, you stop."* (Begin.) After awhile stop it and have the children freeze. Say, *"Look at your fists. If you are a circle or triangle, start dancing when you hear the music. If you are a square or rectangle, stay frozen."* (Begin.) Continue in this manner.

LETTER CARRIER

Cut several circles, triangles, and squares. Put each one in an envelope. Place the letters in a mail sack (tote bag).

Have the children sit in a circle. Ask one child to be the letter carrier. He walks around the outside of the circle with his mail sack. While he's walking, the children say the SHAPE CHANT. When the children say, *"me"* the letter carrier stops and delivers a letter to the child he's standing next to. The child opens it up and tells everyone what shape he received. He walks to the middle of the circle and lays the shape on the floor. The letter carrier gives his mail sack to the next child and the game continues with the children repeating the chant and the new letter carrier delivering another envelope.

SHAPE CHANT

Circles, triangles, squares we see.
What will the letter carrier bring to me?

BOOKS

ED EMBERLEY — *WING ON A FLEA*
— *BOOK ABOUT SHAPES*
TANA HOBAN — *CIRCLES, TRIANGLES, AND SQUARES*
TANA HOBAN — *LOOK AGAIN*
TANA HOBAN — *WHAT IS IT?*

FARM ANIMALS

FOR OPENERS

SING `OLD MCDONALD HAD A FARM' WITH THE CHILDREN. YOU NAME THE FIRST ANIMAL AND THEN LET THE CHILDREN CONTINUE BY NAMING THE ANIMALS THEY WANT ON THEIR FARM. AS YOU ARE SINGING ABOUT EACH ANIMAL, HAVE SEVERAL CHILDREN GO INTO THE MIDDLE AND PRETEND THAT THEY ARE THE ANIMAL. SWITCH CHILDREN AS YOU NAME NEW ANIMALS.

FINGERPLAYS

NAPTIME

"Come little children,"
Calls mother hen.
"It is time to take
Your nap again."

And under her feathers
The small chicks creep
And she clucks a song
Till they fall asleep.
(Using a whisper voice, sing a
favorite song to the sleeping
chicks.)

THE TURKEY

The turkey is a funny bird,
His head goes wobble, wobble,
And all he says is just one word,
"Gobble, gobble, gobble."

FIVE LITTLE DUCKS

Five little ducks that I once knew,
Fat ones, skinny ones, tall ones too,
But the one little duck with the
Feather on his back,

He led the others with a
"Quack, Quack, Quack."
"Quack, Quack, Quack."
"Quack, Quack, Quack."

Down to the river they would go,
Wibble-wobble, wibble-wobble to and fro,
But the one little duck with the
Feather on his back,

He lead the others with a
"Quack, Quack, Quack."
"Quack, Quack, Quack."
"Quack, Quack, Quack."

Up from the river they would come.
Ho, Ho, Ho, Hum, Hum, Hum,
But the one little duck with the
Feather on his back,

He led the others with a
"Quack, Quack, Quack."
"Quack, Quack, Quack."
"Quack, Quack, Quack."

ANIMALS

59

FINGERPLAYS

THE FARMYARD

In the farmyard at the end of the day,
All the animals politely say,
"Thank you for my food today".
The cow says, "Moo".
The pigeon says, "Coo".
The sheep says, "Baa".
The lamb says, "Maa".

The hen says, "Cluck, cluck, cluck".
"Quack", says the duck.
The dog barks, "Bow wow".
The cat says, "Meow".
The horse says, "Neigh".
The pig grunts, "Oink".
Then the barn is locked up tight.
And the farmer says,
"Good Night, Good Night".

60

SNACK

PURPLE COW
YOU'LL NEED:
1/2 cup grape juice
2 cups milk
2 bananas, sliced

TO MAKE: Mix the above ingredients in a blender.
from SUPER SNACKS
by Jean Warren

LANGUAGE GAMES

NAME THE ANIMAL

Make a felt/magnet animal for each child. (There could be duplicates.) Bring the felt/magnet board and the animals to circle time.

Have the children put their hands behind their backs and then quickly go around and give each child one animal. Set up the felt/magnet board for everyone to see. Name one child. Have him secretly look at his animal and then walk towards the board making his animal's noise. The children call out what animal they think he has. He puts it on the board. If they named his animal, the child says, "You guessed it." If they don't, he says, "Guess again." Continue until all of the animals are on the board.

LANGUAGE GAMES

ADD A SOUND

Have a toilet paper roll to use as a telephone. Using the phone, call the person sitting next to you and say a farm animal sound, such as "*Moo.*" That child takes the telephone and calls the person next to him, says the first sound and adds another animal sound. Continue for several more children; then have the next child say all of the animal sounds aloud. Everyone repeat them. Begin the game again.

ANIMAL CHIT-CHAT

Using the animal patterns, make a stick puppet for each animal. Hold two animals, such as a horse and cow, far apart. Start `walking' them towards each other. When they meet, have them stop and `talk.' For example:

COW: "*Hi, friend horse. How are you today?*"

HORSE: "*I'm fine, friend cow. Where are you going?*"

COW: "*I'm going to the barn. It's time for my milking.*"

HORSE: "*I'm going over to the corral to give my friend Rommel a ride.*"

COW: "*Bye, horse.*"

HORSE: "*Bye!*"

Let two children each pick an animal, walk towards each other, and then begin a conversation. When they're done, have them say "*Good-bye*" and walk away. All of the other children clap. Continue with more animal chit-chat.

LANGUAGE GAMES

WHO'S IN THE BARN?

Using posterboard, make all of the farm animals and a simple barn which stands on the floor. Set the barn so that everyone can see it. Hold up each animal and have the children call out what it is.

Now mix them all up and lay them on the floor behind the barn. Pick one animal and hold it behind a barn window so that at least one prominent feature is visible. Have the children guess what animal it is. After they've guessed, bring it out of the barn for the children to see. Name it again. Walk the animal back into the barn. Continue in this manner with the other animals.

FARMER'S SECRET

Put a big handkerchief around your neck and pretend that you're a farmer. Write the names of your farm animals on slips of paper. Put them in your pocket.

Say to the children, "My name is Farmer Chris. I am going to give you clues about my animals and I want you to guess who they are." Pull one slip out of your pocket and give the children clues about that animal. When someone thinks he knows what animal it is, he should call it out. If right say, "You know one of my animals." If they don't, keep giving the children clues. Continue until the children have guessed all of your animals.

ANIMALS

ACTIVE GAMES

MOTHER SAYS   Pretend that you are the `Mother' giving your baby animals different directions:
- "*Mother Turkey says, `Waddle around the barnyard.' (Let them waddle.) `Now gobble as you waddle.'......Stop.*"
- "*Mother Cow says, `Time to come into the barn for dinner. Walk slowly. Talk to each other if you'd like.'......Stop.*"
- "*Mother Horse says, `Let's gallop around the pasture and jump the fences.'......Stop*"
- "*Mother Pig says, `Let's go rolling in the mud. Oink! Oink! Oink! It's so much fun......Time to wash off under the hose.'......Stop.*"
- "*Mother Sheep says, `Get ready for the long walk to the pasture. Exercise your legs.'......Stop.*"

ANIMAL CHASE   Have all of the children sit in a big circle to form the pasture. Have each child name a farm animal he'd like to be and make that animal's noise. (Duplicates are fine.)

Now say to the cows and turkeys, "*Cows and turkeys go to the pasture.*" Children who are these animals get up, and start making animal sounds while chasing each other around the pasture. After a little chasing say, "*Cows and turkeys back to the barn.*" The children sit down. Name two more animals and continue the game.

BOOKS

MARGARET WISE BROWN — *BIG RED BARN*
MARGARET WISE BROWN — *BABY ANIMALS*
MIRRA GINSBURG — *GOOD MORNING MR. CHICK*
JAMES HERRIOT — *BLOSSOM COMES HOME*
ROBERT MUNSCH — *PIGS, PIGS, PIGS*
MEGAN HALSEY LANE — *SOMETHING TO CROW ABOUT*
CHIYOKO NAKATANI — *MY DAY ON THE FARM*
JOAN NODSET — *WHO TOOK THE FARMER'S HATPETS*

ZOO ANIMALS

CUT A FELT/CONSTRUCTION PAPER TREE AND MONKEY. (IF YOU USE CONSTRUCTION PAPER, BACK EACH PIECE WITH MAGNET TAPE.) BRING THEM AND THE FELT/MAGNET BOARD TO CIRCLE TIME.

PUT THE TREE ON THE BOARD. SET THE MONKEY ON A BRANCH. ASK THE CHILDREN, *"WHERE'S THE MONKEY?"* (LET THEM RESPOND.) ASK A CHILD TO PUT THE MONKEY SOMEPLACE ELSE ON THE BOARD, THEN ASK AGAIN, *"WHERE'S THE MONKEY?"* (CHILDREN RESPOND.) KEEP MOVING THE MONKEY AND TALKING ABOUT WHERE HE IS IN RELATION TO THE TREE.

ANIMALS

65

FINGERPLAYS

PRETENDING

I'm a bear - hear me growl!
I'm a lion - hear me roar!
I'm a dog - hear me bark!
I'm an eagle - see me soar!

I'm an elephant - with a trunk.
I'm a camel - with a hump.
I'm a donkey - running races.
I'm a monkey - watch me jump.

AT THE ZOO

I saw a monkey.
I saw a bat.
I saw a green snake.
What do you think of that?

There was a camel,
An elephant, too.
Bears, seals and giraffes,
Are all at the zoo.
  Dick Wilmes

BABY KANGAROO

Jump, jump, jump
Goes the big kangaroo.
I thought there was one,
But now I see two.

The mother takes her young one
Along in a pouch,
Where he can nap,
Like a child on a couch.

Jump, jump, jump.
Goes the mother kangaroo
Wherever she goes,
Her baby goes, too.

SNACK

MONKEY MEAL
YOU'LL NEED:
Hot dog buns
Peanut butter
Bananas

TO MAKE: Peel the bananas.
Spread peanut butter in the
bun and put in a banana.
Cut the `monkey meals' in
half and serve.

LANGUAGE GAMES

WHICH ONE DOESN'T BELONG?

Say a series of words all but one of which are zoo animals, such as *"elephant, monkey, box, lion, seal."* Then say to the children, *"Which one doesn't belong?"* The children call out the non-animal word, in this case, *"box."* Continue with different series of words.

WHO'S THE LION?

Have one child sit in a chair with his back to the group and cover his eyes. He's the `lion tamer.' Tap a second child on the head. That child makes a lion sound. The child in the chair turns around and guesses who the lion is. If he was right, the lion lets out a loud roar and trades places with the child in the chair; if not, he turns back around and the lion lets out another roar, so the child can guess again. Continue in this manner.

LOOK CAREFULLY

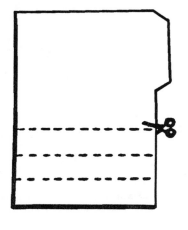

Make `Zoo Animal Peek-A-Boo' folders. Get a file folder and a picture of a zoo animal. Open the folder and glue the picture on the right side. Close the folder. On the front cover rule off 8, 11/2" strips. Cut each strip. Make 7 or 8 more folders, using other zoo animals.

Bring the `Peek-A-Boo' folders to circle time. Hold up one folder. Tell the children that a zoo animal is hiding in the folder and they are going to try and figure out who it is. They should look carefully as you slowly open each strip. Open one strip. What do the children see? Can anyone guess what animal it is? Continue, revealing more parts of the animal until the children can name the animal. Repeat with the other `Peek-A-Boo' folders.

ANIMALS

LANGUAGE GAMES

VISIT THE ZOO   Cut a giant elephant out of posterboard. Bring it and a marker to circle time. Ask the children, *"If we were going to the zoo what animals would we see?"* As they name the animals, write them on the elephant. Hang the elephant at their eye level. Add to it as the children think of more animals.

REMEMBER THE ANIMALS   Get 7 or 8 different stuffed animals — maybe the children can bring them from home. Set them on the floor for everyone to see. Point to each one and have the children tell what it is. Collect all of the animals and set them in a large box. Have the children call out one of the animals they remember. Take it out of the box and set it where everyone can see it. Have the children name another animal, take it out, and set it on the floor. Continue trying to remember all of the animals.

ACTIVE GAMES

ACT LIKE AN ANIMAL

Have the children stand in a circle with room in the middle. Have one child come to you and whisper a zoo animal in your ear. Then say, *"Jerome, act like a _____."* The child starts acting like the animal he named. Then say, *"Everyone act like a _____."* (Do it.) *"Stop."* Have another child whisper an animal name in your ear and continue playing the game.

FOLLOW THE LEADER

Have the children line-up behind you. Start walking like an elephant. They should follow you all pretending to be elephants. Change to another animal and let the children keep copying you. (penguin, snake, monkey, gorilla, bat, etc.)

ANIMAL HUNT

Hide pictures of zoo animals around the room — at least one for each child. When you say, *"Go,"* have the children search the room for pictures. When a child finds one, he should pick it up and come back to the circle time area. Have each child turn his picture over and put it behind him. Call on each child to pretend to be his animal. Others should call out what animal it is.

BOOKS

RUTH HELLER — *ANIMALS BORN ALIVE*
DAVID MCPHAIL — *THE BEAR'S TOOTHACHE*
BILL MARTIN — *POLAR BEAR, POLAR BEAR WHAT DO YOU HEAR?*
BILL MARTIN — *BROWN BEAR, BROWN BEAR WHAT DO YOU SEE?*
JEFF SHEPPARD — *THE RIGHT NUMBER OF ELEPHANTS*
ESPHYR SLOBODKINA — *CAPS FOR SALE*
MASAYUKI YABUUCHI — *WHOSE BABY?*

ANIMALS

PETS

FOR OPENERS

USING THE PATTERNS MAKE POSTERBOARD PETS. CUT EACH PET INTO 2 OR 3 PIECES. PUT MAGNET TAPE ON THE BACK OF EACH PIECE.

BRING THE PET PUZZLES AND A MAGNET BOARD TO CIRCLE TIME. (MAGNETIC DRY ERASE BOARDS AND COUNTER TOP PROTECTORS MAKE GOOD MAGNET BOARDS.) PASS OUT THE PUZZLE PIECES TO THE CHILDREN. HAVE THEM LOOK AT THEIR PIECES AND TRY TO DECIDE WHICH PET PIECE THEY MIGHT HAVE. GO AROUND THE GROUP AND HAVE EACH CHILD SHARE WHAT PET HE THINKS HE HAS AND WHY HE THINKS IT IS THAT PARTICULAR ONE.

ASK ONE CHILD TO PUT HIS PIECE ON THE MAGNET BOARD. HAVE THE OTHERS LOOK AT THEIR PIECES. WHO MIGHT HAVE A PIECE TO THE SAME PET? LET THE CHILDREN TRY. IF A PIECE FITS, LEAVE IT AND NAME THE PET; IF NOT, THE CHILD SHOULD KEEP HIS PIECE. CONTINUE UNTIL ALL OF THE PET PUZZLES ARE ON THE MAGNET BOARD.

ANIMALS

71

FINGERPLAYS

KITTENS

Five little kittens
Sleeping on a chair.
One rolled off,
Leaving four there.

Four little kittens,
One climbed a tree,
To look in a bird's nest.
Then there were three.

Three little kittens
Wondered what to do.
One saw a mouse,
Then there were two.

Two little kittens
Playing near a wall.
One little kitten
Chased a red ball.

One little kitten
With fur soft as silk,
Left all alone
To drink a dish of milk.

LITTLE PUPPIES AND KITTENS

One little, two little, three little kittens,
Were napping in the sun.
One little, two little, three little puppies said,
"Come, let us all have fun."

Up to the kittens the puppies went creeping,
As quiet as quiet could be.
One little, two little, three little kittens
Went scampering up a tall tree.

LET'S PRETEND

Let's pretend we're having fun
At a picnic everyone.

Then some picnic pets come 'round.
Birds that flutter to the ground.

Crickets who can jump so funny,
And a wiggly little bunny.

Butterflies on lazy wings,
Squirrels and lots of other things!

Let's pretend that we are all
Picnic pets who have come to call.
  Dick Wilmes

(Let children choose a picnic pet and fly,
hop, jump, or run around the room.)

SNACK

WATER
YOU'LL NEED:
Tap water
Soda water
Mineral water
Distilled water

TO MAKE: Pour the different types of water into glasses.
Let the children drink the water. Discuss the differences.

CLASSROOM VISITOR

- On a special day have the children bring their favorite stuffed animals from home. Let the special pets join all of the daily activities.

LANGUAGE GAMES

CAT IN THE HAT Get plastic pet figures and put them in a hat so no-one can see them. Pull one out, set it on the floor and have the children call out what it is. Continue until all of the pets are lined up. Have the children cover their eyes. Put one pet back into the hat. Have the children uncover their eyes and name the animal which you put back in the hat. Continue until all of the pets are in the hat.

WHO AM I? Make the sound of a pet and have the children call out which one they think it is. Duplicate some of the pet sounds using soft, loud, squeaky, hoarse, etc. voices.

POLLY WANTS A CRACKER Make a `Polly Parrot' stick puppet by gluing a magazine picture of a parrot to a tongue depressor. Hold Polly up and let her give the children orders. After each one be sure to feed *Polly* a cracker.

- *"Polly wants everyone to sing THE WHEELS ON THE BUS."* (Sing and then pretend to give Polly a cracker.)
- *"Polly wants Elizabeth, Angel, and Jesse to stand and jump up and down."* (cracker)
- *"Polly wants Darwin to shake hands with Jim."* (cracker)
- Continue with additional directions.

LANGUAGE GAMES

ANIMAL CATCHER

Using the patterns make lots of colored construction paper pets. Slip a metal paper clip on each one. Make 2 or 3 'leashes' by tying magnets to the ends of 3' pieces of twine.

   Give several children the leashes. Tell each animal catcher what pet you want him to catch, such as *"Nicole catch the green bird."* She uses her leash to catch the pet. When she gets it everyone claps for her. She gives the pet to you for safe keeping and hands her leash to a friend. You tell the new animal catcher what pet to catch. Continue until all of the pets have been caught.

VISIT THE PET STORE

Begin telling the children a story about a visit to the pet store. Let them add to the story as it develops. You could begin as follows:

   One day I thought it would be great to have a pet, so I decided to visit a pet store. I drove down the street and parked in front of the store. I walked in and said, "Hi" to Mrs. Peet. She said, "Hi, how can I help you, Ashley?" (Let the children continue. Talk about all of the pets that might be in the pet store.)

ACTIVE GAMES

CATS AND DOGS

Divide the group into cats and dogs. Have the dogs hold hands and the cats go into the middle. When you say, "Cats and dogs play," the dogs raise up their arms and bark while the cats run in and out as they meow. When you say, "Cats and dogs rest," the dogs put their arms down and the cats lie on the floor. All of the animals should be quiet. When you say, "Cats and dogs play," the dogs hold up their arms again and the cats begin running. After several times switch the dogs and cats.

IN THE DOGHOUSE

Using a long clothesline, make a giant square on the floor to represent the doghouse. Have the children pretend to be puppies learning how to play in and out of the doghouse.

- "Puppies, hop into the doghouse."
- "Puppies, crawl out of the doghouse."
- "Puppies, march around the outside of the doghouse."
- "Puppies, tiptoe into the doghouse."
- "Puppies, jump up and down in your doghouse."
- "Puppies, skip out of your doghouse."

Continue.

Last one, "Puppies, lie down in your doghouse."

BOOKS

CHARLIE ANDERSON — *CATS, DOGS AND OTHER PETS*
LORNA BALIAN — *AMELIA'S NINE LIVES*
TERRENCE BLACKER — *HERBIE, WHERE ARE YOU?*
NORMAN BRIDWELL — *CLIFFORD'S BIRTHDAY PARTY*
ALEXANDRA DAY — *CARL GOES SHOPPING*
EZRA JACK KEATS — *HI, CAT!*
EZRA JACK KEATS — *PET SHOW*
NORMA SIMON — *CATS DO, DOGS DON'T*
NORMA SIMON — *WHERE DOES MY CAT SLEEP?*

ANIMALS

INSECTS, SPIDERS, BUGS

FOR OPENERS

HAVE THE CHILDREN SING AND DO THE ACTIONS FOR `THE EENCY, WEENCY SPIDER` SEVERAL TIMES, EACH TIME PRETENDING TO BE A DIFFERENT TYPE OF SPIDER, MOVING IN A DIFFERENT WAY:

- SING THE ORIGINAL WORDS IN A NORMAL VOICE, PORTRAYING A REGULAR SPIDER `WALKING` UP THE SPOUT.

- SING IN A TINY VOICE, PORTRAYING A BABY SPIDER `CRAWLING` UP THE SPOUT.

- SING IN A HUSKY VOICE, PORTRAYING A BIG, FAT SPIDER `LUMBERING` UP THE SPOUT.

- SING IN A WHISPER VOICE, PORTRAYING A SNEAKY SPIDER `TIPTOEING` UP THE SPOUT.

THE EENCY WEENCY SPIDER

THE EENCY WEENCY SPIDER
WENT UP THE WATER SPOUT. (Walk fingers up arm.)

OUT CAME THE RAIN (Wiggle fingers like rain.)
AND WASHED THE SPIDER OUT. (Spread arms apart.)

OUT CAME THE SUN (Make circle with arms.)
AND DRIED UP ALL THE RAIN,

AND THE EENCY WEENCY SPIDER (Walk fingers up arms again.)
CRAWLED UP THE SPOUT AGAIN.

FINGERPLAYS

BEEHIVE

Here is the beehive.
Where are the bees?
Hidden away where nobody sees,
Soon they come creeping out of the hive.
One, two, three, four, five.

ANT HILL

Once I saw an ant hill
With no ants about.
So I said, "Dear little ants,
Won't you come out?"

Then, as if the little ants
Had heard my call,
One, two, three, four, five came out!
And began climbing the wall

1, 2, 3

1,2,3, there's a bug on me!
Where did he go! I don't know!

TAKING A WALK

Taking a walk,
Was so much fun,
We didn't hurry,
We didn't run.'

We looked at all,
The lovely trees.
We watched for birds,
And watched for bees.

SNACK

PLAYDOUGH HIVES
YOU'LL NEED:
1 18 ounce jar of peanut butter
6t honey
2-3 cups of non-fat dry milk (enough to give
    the mixture a doughy consistency)
Raisins

TO MAKE: Mix all of the ingredients together. Let the children make hives, cocoons, and anthills with the mixture and then add raisin bugs.

FIELD TRIP

- Take a walk to a nearby park or around your neighborhood. Find a large tree or several small ones. Quietly stand by your tree and look at it carefully. See if you can find any insects or spiders. Watch them. What are they doing?

ANIMALS

LANGUAGE GAMES

WE LIKE INSECTS Make an *INSECT STRIP* by duplicating each of the insect pictures and gluing them to a 5"x28" strip of posterboard. Point to each one and tell the children what type of bug it is. Repeat and let the children name them.

Now have a child come up and point to his favorite insect and tell why he likes it. Who else likes that bug and why? Have another child point to a bug and tell why he likes that one best. Continue talking about the insects.

LITTLE MISS MUFFET Have the children sit in a circle. Put a chair in the middle. Have one child be Little Miss Muffet and sit on the chair. Name a second child be the spider.

Say the *LITTLE MISS MUFFET* rhyme. As you do, Miss Muffet should be eating. When you say the line about the spider, the child who is the spider should crawl over to her and sit down next to her. Miss Muffet gets scared and runs away.

The spider becomes Miss Muffet and sits in the chair. Name another spider. Let that spider choose where to sit (under, behind, in front of, or beside). When he's sitting, have the children finish the line describing where the spider chose to sit and continue with the rhyme. Repeat with more spiders.

LADYBUG COUNT Make 11 construction paper ladybugs with zero to ten spots on them. Back each one with felt/magnet tape. Bring the ladybugs and felt/magnet board to circle time.

Put a ladybug on the board. Count the spots with the children. Repeat with the other bugs.

Put all of the ladybugs on the board. Arrange them in order from 0 to 10 — backwards from 10 to 0.

Put several ladybugs on the board. Count the bugs. Then count how many spots they have all together. Repeat with other sets of bugs.

Beetle

Ladybug

Ant

Spider

Mosquito

Fly

ANIMALS

LANGUAGE GAMES

TELL WHAT YOU KNOW

Make the *INSECT STRIP* described in `We Like Insects` and bring it to circle time. Point to one of the insects and name it. Have the children tell each other everything they know about it — color, how it moves, size, where it lives, etc.

BUG IN THE RUG

Have the children sit around the edges of a blanket/sheet. Choose a child to stand with his back to the group. Then one of the children should crawl under the blanket/sheet. The children sitting around the blanket/sheet should chant:

Bug in the rug
Bug in the rug
Who is that
Bug in the rug?

The child who is standing, turns around, looks at all of the children and tries to guess who is missing. If he needs help to figure it out, the `bug` makes a `bug noise` and the child guesses again. When guessed, the `bug` crawls out and sits in the circle.

ACTIVE GAMES

BEE STING

Have one child be the bee. He buzzes around trying to `sting` the others. When he touches or stings a child, that child becomes a bee, and begins buzzing around with the first bee trying to `sting` more children. Keep playing until everyone is stung and is buzzing around.

BUGGY WUGGY

Do the *HOKEY POKEY* with the children substituting insect and spider body parts for the original human parts in the lyrics — *"Put your feelers in...Put your wings in...stingers...backbones...legs...etc.*
Vohny Moehling

BOOKS

RUTH BROWN — *THE BIG SNEEZE*
ARTHUR DORROS — *ANT CITIES*
ERIC CARLE — *THE VERY BUSY SPIDER*
ERIC CARLE — *THE VERY QUIET CRICKET*
ERIC CARLE — *GROUCHY LADYBUG*
KIYSHI SOYA — *A HOUSE OF LEAVES*
NANCY WINSLOW — *BUGS*

WORMS

FOR OPENERS

EARTHWORMS MOVE ALONG THE GROUND BY CONTRACTING TWO KINDS OF MUSCLES. HAVE THE CHILDREN PRETEND THAT THEIR POINTER FINGERS ARE WORMS AND IT'S TIME FOR `WORM EXERCISES.'

- *"WORMS, MOVE SLOWLY ALONG THE GROUND."*
- *"WORMS, BURROW OUT OF THE GROUND....DIG BACK IN."*
- *"WORMS, STAND AT ATTENTION AND `STREEEEETCH' TALL."*
- *"WORMS, SLOWLY ROLL INTO A BALL....STRETCH OUT AGAIN."*
- *"WORMS, WIGGLE QUICKLY ALONG THE GROUND."*
- *"WORMS, CRAWL ALONG UNTIL YOU MEET A FRIEND. TALK TO YOUR FRIEND....HUG YOUR FRIEND....WAVE GOOD-BYE TO YOUR FRIEND."*
- *"WORMS, WIGGLE BACKWARDS."*
- CONTINUE.
- LAST ONE. *"WORMS, TAKE A REST."*

FINGERPLAYS

DIRT

Dirt comes in colors,
Black, red, and brown.
It makes a home for animals,
Living in the ground.

Worms, snakes, ants, and bugs
Live beneath my shoe.
If there wasn't dirt between us
I wouldn't know what to do.
  Dick Wilmes

A ROBIN

When a robin cocks his head,
Sideways in a flower bed,
He can hear the tiny sound
Of a worm beneath the ground.

SNACK

WORM SANDWICHES
YOU'LL NEED:
Sliced wheat/pumpernickel bread
Peanut butter

TO MAKE: Let the children use spoons to squiggle peanut butter worms on the dark bread. Enjoy with glasses milk.

FIELD TRIPS

- Just after a rain, when the worms are moving around the sidewalks, take the children for a walk. Look for the worms. Talk about their size, color, movements, and so on. Find the longest, fattest, shortest, thinnest, wiggliest ones.
- Make an appointment and visit the local bait shop. Have the clerk give the children a tour of the shop, talk about where the worms come from, and how they are transported.

LANGUAGE GAMES

WALK WITH A WORM

Glue a pipe cleaner or construction paper worm to a twig. Hold the worm and begin telling a story about his walk around your neighborhood. After you've begun, pass the worm to someone else and let him add to the story. Continue passing the worm around and expanding the story. You could start like this:

WALK WITH A WORM
"It just stopped raining so I think I'll crawl out and see what's going on above the ground. (Wiggle, wiggle, wiggle.) The sun is very bright. I better put on my sunglasses. I know the children will be out soon. They love to splash in the puddles after a rain...."
(Pass the worm.)

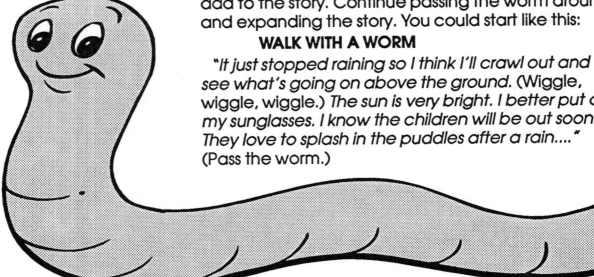

82

LANGUAGE GAMES

HOW MANY?   Cut out 10 felt worms. Put a certain number on the felt board. Point to each one and count together. After counting, ask how many worms there are. Repeat using different sets of worms.

FAT WORMS,   Using felt or construction paper, make lots of fat and
SKINNY WORMS   skinny worms. If you used construction paper, back your worms with magnet tape. Bring the worms and your felt/magnet board to circle time.

Put all of your worms on the bottom of the board. Put a fat worm at the top left side of the board and a skinny one on the right side. Have a child come up, pick a worm, decide if it is fat or skinny and then put it on the appropriate side of the board. Continue sorting the worms until all of the fat ones are on one side and the skinny ones are on the other side.

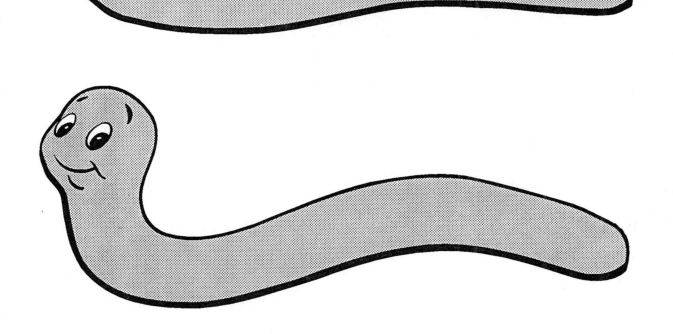

ACTIVE GAMES

PARACHUTE PLAY

Cut a clothesline into 4 or 5 three foot lengths. Have the children stand around the parachute. Put one worm' on the chute. Let the children help him burrow into the ground by gently wiggling the chute so that he moves towards the hole and then crawls through. As you're wiggling the chute, slowly chant over and over:

Wiggle worm, wiggle worm
Wiggle, wiggle, wiggle.

Repeat the activity using 2 to 3 worms and then all of the worms. (HELPFUL HINT: Before playing ask one child to be the worm catcher. When a worm/s crawls through the hole, the catcher goes under the chute and gets the worm/s. The rest of the children hold the chute up high.)

WIGGLING WORM

Teach the children this chant and let their whole bodies be worms and move accordingly.

WIGGLING WORM

Wiggling worm, wiggling worm,
Wiggle, wiggle, wiggle.

Marching worm, marching worm,
March, march, march.

Crawling worm

Hopping worm

Continue with other movements the children create for `Wiggling Worm' ending with

Sleeping worm, sleeping worm,
Sleep, sleep, sleep.

Snoring worm, snoring worm,
Snore, snore, snore.

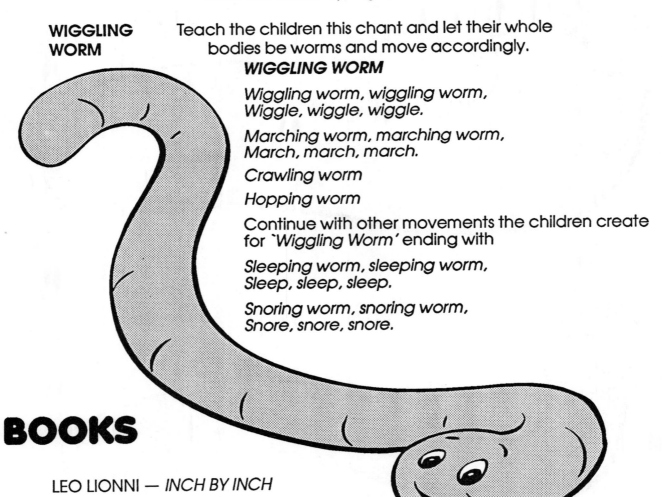

BOOKS

LEO LIONNI — *INCH BY INCH*

CATERPILLARS/BUTTERFLIES

FOR OPENERS

MAKE A `SIMPLE STAGES OF THE BUTTERFLY' POSTERBOARD BOOK TO READ TO YOUR CHILDREN. USE THE ILLUSTRATION AS A GUIDE. AFTER `READING' THE PICTURES TO THEM, PUT THE BOOK ON YOUR BOOKSHELF OR STAND IT ON A LOW SHELF.
Dawn Zavodsky

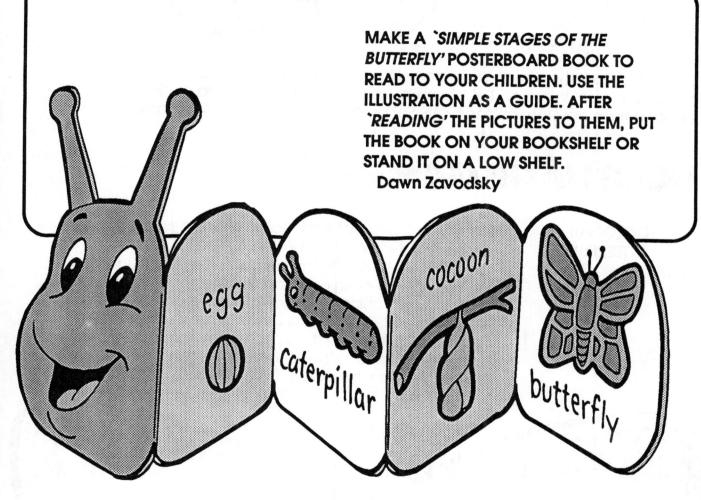

FINGERPLAYS

FUZZY WUZZY CATERPILLAR

Fuzzy wuzzy caterpillar
Into a corner will creep,
He'll spin himself a blanket,
And then go fast asleep,

Fuzzy wuzzy caterpillar
Wakes up by and by
To find he has wings of beauty
And has changed to a butterfly.

CATERPILLARS, CATERPILLARS
(Adapted from traditional rhyme.)

Caterpillars, caterpillars,
Will you come out? (Thumbs in fists.)
Yes we will. (Pop thumbs out.)
But we are butterflies,
And will fly about. (Fly thumbs around.)

SNACK

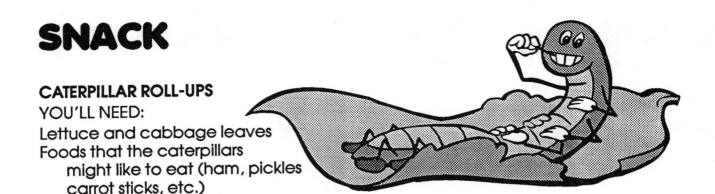

CATERPILLAR ROLL-UPS

YOU'LL NEED:

Lettuce and cabbage leaves
Foods that the caterpillars
    might like to eat (ham, pickles
    carrot sticks, etc.)

TO MAKE: Wash the leaves and spread them out flat. Have the different caterpillar foods in dishes. Let the children choose which food to put in each leaf and then carefully roll them up. Set on a plate and serve with crackers.

LANGUAGE GAMES

COLORFUL BUTTERFLIES

Using the butterfly pattern, make different colored butterflies. Teach your children *CATERPILLARS, CATERPILLARS* with the movements. Lay the butterflies on the floor so everyone can see them.

At the beginning of the rhyme have one child go into the middle, choose a butterfly, and start flying around with it. When the children say the fourth line of the rhyme, have them name the color of the butterfly which the child is flying. Repeat with other butterflies.

LANGUAGE GAMES

IMAGINATION STRETCHER

Tell the children to pretend that they are caterpillars in their cocoons changing into butterflies. Ask them, *"What are you thinking about in your cocoons?"*

MAKE A CATERPILLAR

Cut a felt caterpillar head and 10, 21/2" felt orange and black circles. Bring the caterpillar's pieces and the felt board to circle time.

Put the caterpillar's head on the felt board. Add felt circles in a certain pattern such as orange, black, orange, black, orange, black. Say the pattern aloud with the children. Have them continue it by adding several more circles. Remove the circles and make a new caterpillar with a different pattern: orange-orange-black, orange-orange-black, orange.... Continue by creating different caterpillars.

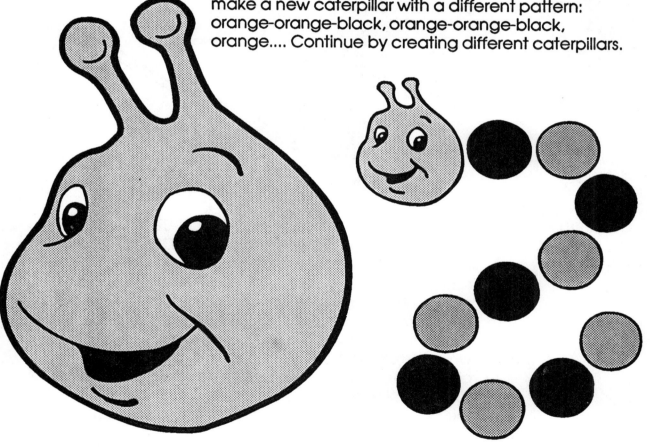

WHICH ONE DOESN'T BELONG

Slowly say a series of words, all but one of which are things a butterfly might see as he's flying around, such as *"tree, sidewalk, clouds, desk, mailbox, weeds."* Then say, *"Which one doesn't belong?"* The children say the one which a butterfly would not see and why. Repeat using a different series.

87

ACTIVE GAMES

STOP, WATCH, AND FLY

Give 2 colored streamers for butterfly wings to each child and yourself. Pretend you're all butterflies and fly around the room, getting used to your new wings.

After a little flying, squat down as if landing on a flower. All of the butterflies do the same. Rest for a moment. Then you take off flying in a special way, such as on your tiptoes, moving your wings quickly or slowly, in swooping fashion, and so on. (Children follow.) Squat on another flower to rest and then take off again using a different motion. Repeat with several different movements and then let the children create their own butterfly movements for the others to follow.

CATERPILLAR, CATERPILLAR, BUTTERFLY

Have the children in a circle and play *CATERPILLAR, CATERPILLAR, BUTTERFLY*, a variation of *DUCK, DUCK, GOOSE*. Pick one child to begin. This child is the caterpillar and he wiggles around the circle tapping each child on the shoulder until he gets to the child he wants to chase him. He taps that child and says, *"Butterfly."* The first child wiggles as quickly as he can while the child who is the butterfly, flies around the circle trying to catch him before he gets back to his space. While the butterfly is chasing the caterpillar, the other children encourage them by clapping.

BOOKS

RUTH BROWN — *IF AT FIRST YOU DO NOT SEE*
ERIC CARLE — *VERY HUNGRY CATERPILLAR*
MAY GARELICK — *WHERE DOES THE BUTTERFLY GO WHEN IT RAINS?*
BARRIE WATTS — *BUTTERFLY AND CATERPILLAR*

BIRDS

FOR OPENERS

PLAY A `YES' - `NO' GAME WITH THE CHILDREN. CUT OUT PICTURES OF DIFFERENT BIRDS AND OTHER ANIMALS FROM MAGAZINES. CUT TWO 3"x6" POSTERBOARD CARDS. WRITE *"YES"* ON ONE CARD AND *"NO"* ON THE OTHER CARD. BACK EACH PICTURE AND CARD WITH A PIECE OF MAGNET TAPE OR FELT. BRING THE PICTURES, CARDS, AND THE FELT/MAGNET BOARD TO CIRCLE TIME.

PUT THE `YES' AND `NO' CARDS AT THE TOP OF THE BOARD. SHOW THE CHILDREN EACH PICTURE AND HAVE THEM CALL OUT *"YES"* IF IT IS A BIRD PICTURE AND *"NO"* IF IT IS ANOTHER TYPE OF ANIMAL. LET ONE CHILD COME UP AND PLACE THE PICTURE UNDER THE `YES' OR `NO' CARD. (HELP IF NECESSARY.) CONTINUE UNTIL ALL OF THE PICTURES ARE ON THE BOARD.

POINT TO ALL OF THE BIRD PICTURES AND HAVE THE CHILDREN CALL OUT WHAT EACH ONE IS. REPEAT WITH THE PICTURES OF THE OTHER ANIMALS.

FINGERPLAYS

BIRD TALK

Birds fly through the sky,
Above the trees, oh so high,
Chirping loudly through the day,
I wonder what they have to say.
  Dick Wilmes

FIVE LITTLE BIRDS

Five little birds without any home,
Five little trees in a row.
Come build your nests in our
branches tall,
We'll rock you to and fro.

IF I WERE A BIRD

If I were a bird,
I would learn to fly,
Twisting and turning,
All over the sky.

Up to the clouds,
Down to the ground,
Stretching my wings,
As I turned all around.

Come pretend
And fly with me,
Up to our home
In the top of a tree.
  Dick Wilmes

ANIMALS

SNACK

BIRD NESTS
YOU'LL NEED:
6T margarine
6 cups miniature marshmallows
1t vanilla
1/2t each, red and green food coloring
8 cups of Cheerios

TO MAKE: Melt the margarine and marshmallows together, stirring constantly. Remove from the heat and add the food coloring and vanilla. Fold in the Cheerios. Cool and then let the children form bird nests. Could add tiny cream cheese ball eggs to the nests.

CLASSROOM VISITOR

● Call your local nature organization or Audobon Society. Arrange for one of the members to visit your class and tell the children some easy facts about birds. Suggest that the visitor bring slides or posters to show the children.
    Take a walk around the neighborhood with your visitor. Everyone watch and listen for birds.

LANGUAGE GAMES

TWO LITTLE BLACKBIRDS

Make pairs of black bird finger puppets. Say the *TWO LITTLE BLACKBIRDS* rhyme, letting the finger puppets do the motions along with the children.

TWO LITTLE BLACKBIRDS
Two little blackbirds sitting on the hill.
        (Thumbs in fists.)
One named Jack, one named Jill.
        (Hold thumbs up.)
Fly away Jack, fly away Jill.
        (Fly behind back.)
Fly back Jack, fly back Jill.
        (Fly birds back.)

Repeat the rhyme changing the third and fourth lines so that Jack and Jill move in different ways: hop away, swoop away, fly fast away, and other movements that the children suggest.

LANGUAGE GAMES

HOW MANY BABIES?

Make a felt nest, bird, and 10 eggs. Bring them along with the felt board to circle time. Put the nest on the board. Have the children cover their eyes. Set some eggs in the nest and let Mother Bird sit on them. Have the children uncover their eyes and then say to them, *"How many babies will Mrs. Bird, hatch?"* Take Mother Bird off of the eggs. Point to each egg and count them together. Repeat using different amounts of eggs.

BIRDS ARE BORN

Duplicate the sequence pictures. Glue each one to lightweight cardboard and laminate or cover them with clear adhesive paper. Attach a popsicle stick to the backside of each one.

Give the sequence cards to four different children. Have them stand, in mixed up order, in a row holding the cards out in front of them. Have the other children look at the pictures and arrange them in order by finding the child holding the first picture and having him stand first in line, the child holding the second picture stand second in line, and so on.

ANIMALS

91

LANGUAGE GAMES

TWEET, TWEET　Talk to the children in bird talk, using a specific pattern of tweets, such as whispering, "*tweet, tweet, tweet,*" and having them echo it back. Repeat, using different patterns.
EXTENSION:
Use other bird languages such as the turkey's `gobble' and the duck's `quack.'

ACTIVE GAMES

FLY AND SPY　Have the children pretend that they are birds about ready to take off from the tree. "*Flap your wings and start flying around the sky.*" (Let the children fly.) Say, "*Stop, birds.*" The birds should stop where they are and look around. Let several birds tell what they see. Then say, "*Fly on, birds.*" After awhile have them stop again and talk about what they see. (Continue.)

BIRDS OF A FEATHER FLOCK TOGETHER

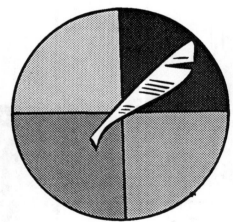

Make a spinner board with at least 4 different colors. Make very simple bird headbands for the children, each with one colored feather to match one of the colors on the spinner board.

Give each child a headband, have him name the color of his feather, and then put it on. After all of the children are wearing their headbands, flick the spinner and wait until it stops on a color. Say, "*Red birds, fly high in the sky.*" (Redbirds fly around.) Continue playing by flicking the spinner and giving directions to other flocks of birds, such as:
"*Blue birds, fly around and look for worms.*"
"*Green and yellow birds fly around and then land in your nests.*"
"*Blue birds, soar around the sky.*"

BOOKS

MICHAEL FOREMAN — *CAT AND CANARY*
MIRRA GINSBURG — *CHICK AND THE DUCKLING*
HELEN LESTER — *TACKY THE PENGUIN*
LEO LIONNI — *TICO AND THE GOLDEN WINGS*
ROBERT McCLOSKEY — *MAKE WAY FOR DUCKLINGS*
ANNE ROCKWELL — *MY SPRING ROBIN*

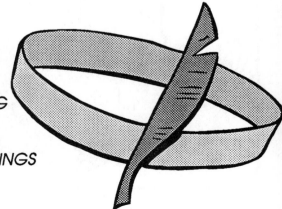

VEGETABLES

FOR OPENERS

CUT OUT A GIANT GARDEN SHOVEL FROM A PIECE OF POSTERBOARD. BRING IT AND A MARKER TO CIRCLE TIME. READ THIS RHYME TO THE CHILDREN:

VEGETABLE GARDEN

I HAVE A SPECIAL PIECE OF LAND,
JUST OUTSIDE MY DOOR.
IT'S GOING TO BE A GARDEN,
WITH VEGETABLES GALORE.

DICK WILMES

HAVE THE CHILDREN BEGIN NAMING VEGETABLES THAT THEY COULD GROW IN THEIR GARDENS. LIST THE VEGETABLES ON THE SHOVEL. HANG THE LIST AT THE CHILDREN'S EYE LEVEL AND ADD TO IT AS THEY THINK OF MORE VEGETABLES.

FINGERPLAYS

GARDENER AND HIS SEEDS
(tune: The Farmer In the Dell)

The gardener plants his seeds,
The gardener plants his seeds,
Hi, ho the derry-o,
The gardener plants his seeds.

The sun comes out to shine, etc.

The rain begins to fall, etc.

The seeds begin to grow, etc.

The gardener picks his vegetables, etc.

He puts them in a basket, etc.

We'll have them all for dinner, etc.

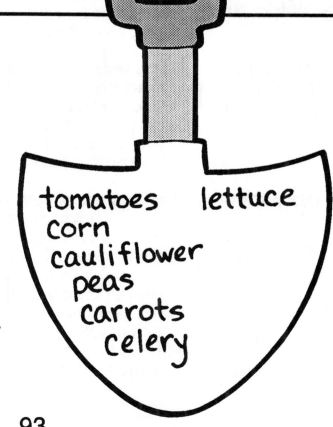

tomatoes   lettuce
corn
cauliflower
peas
carrots
celery

F
O
O
D
S

93

SNACK

VEGETABLE SAMPLER
YOU'LL NEED

Carrot, sweet potato
Radish, tomato
Squash, corn

Cauliflower, cucumber
Broccoli, celery

TO MAKE: Each day
serve a different
colored vegetable.

LANGUAGE GAMES

PLANT YOUR GARDEN

Cut out pairs of 10 to 15 different vegetables. Get a piece of brown or black posterboard. Plant your garden by gluing one vegetable from each pair to the posterboard. (Leave space between each vegetable for matching.) Make vegetable cards by gluing each mate to a piece of lightweight cardboard. Laminate or cover each one with clear adhesive paper.

Bring the vegetable garden and cards to circle time. Hold up the garden, and point to and name each vegetable. Lay the garden on the floor. Pass out the cards. Have a child name one of the vegetables in the garden. Everyone look at his card. If he has that vegetable have him come to the garden and plant his vegetable next to the first one. Continue naming and matching vegetables until the garden is completely planted.

VEGETABLE ECHO

Name several vegetables and have the children echo them back. Now have a child name a vegetable and everyone else echo it back to him. Continue naming and echoing vegetables. Make the game a little more challenging by naming 2 or 3 vegetables and having the children echo them back.

TALK ABOUT

Get a variety of fresh vegetables. Put them in a basket. Hold each one up, let the children name it, and lay it on a tray. After all of the vegetables have been named, have a child come, pick up a vegetable, and hold it for everyone to see. Look at it and let the children tell everything they know about it. Then have the child put it back into the basket.
EXTENSION:
Have bite-size pieces of each vegetable ready to sample. After talking about each one, taste it.

ACTIVE GAMES

PLANT A VEGETABLE Get small cups, dirt, and several types of vegetable seeds, such as peppers, tomatoes, and peas. Plant the seeds with the children. Put their names on their cups. Place all of the cups on a tray and set them in the window. Water and turn them regularly. After they've sprouted, transplant them into your classroom garden or have the children take them home to re-plant.

ACTIVE GAMES

UNDER GROUND, ABOVE GROUND You be the gardener taking a walk through your garden. Have the children pretend that they are the vegetables growing in your garden. If the vegetables grow underground, the children should squat as low as they can and cover their heads; if the vegetables grow above ground, the children should stand and stretch high. As you walk, talk aloud giving the children directions.

- *"Here are my tomatoes growing above the ground. (Children stretch high.) They are changing from green to red. Pretty soon they will be ready to pick."*

- *"Look, here are the green peppers growing above the ground. (Children stretch some more.) They look too small to pick."*

- *"The onions are next. They are under the ground. (Squat and cover head.) I love to eat onions on my hamburgers."*

- Continue the walk:

ABOVE	BELOW
Peas	Carrots
Beans	Beets
Corn	Potatoes
Lettuce	Radishes

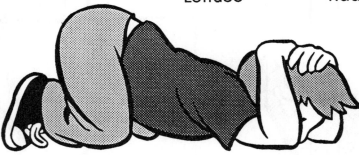

BOOKS

ALIKI - *CORN IS MAIZE*
THOMAS BERGER - *THE MOUSE AND THE POTATO*
MARCIA BROWN - *STONE SOUP*
LOIS EHLERT - *GROWING VEGETABLE SOUP*
RUTH KRAUSS - *THE CARROT SEED*
BEATRIX POTTER - *THE TALE OF PETER RABBIT*

POTATOES

CUT OUT 10 LARGE POTATO SHAPES FROM POSTERBOARD. WRITE THE NUMERALS FROM 1-10 ON THEM. TEACH YOUR CHILDREN THE `ONE POTATO' RHYME. NOW PASS OUT THE POTATOES. SLOWLY SAY THE RHYME. AS YOU SAY EACH NUMBER, HAVE THE CHILD HOLDING THAT POTATO STAND AND STAY STANDING UNTIL THE END. AT THE END EVERYONE LET OUT A ROAR AND SIT BACK DOWN. SWITCH THE POTATOES AROUND AND PLAY AGAIN.

ONE POTATO
(Adapted from traditional rhyme)

One potato, two potato
Three potato, four.
Five potato, six potato
Seven potato, more.
Eight potato, nine potato
Ten potato, more
Let out a roar (Everyone roar!)
Sit back on the floor.
  Liz Wilmes

FOODS

97

FINGERPLAYS

MY GARDEN
Here is a tiny brown potato seed.
I'll plant it in my garden bed.
Down comes the rain to water it,
While the sun shines overhead.

SNACK

POTATO SALAD
Bring the boiled potatoes to school. Let the children use plastic knives to cut up the potatoes. Prepare the other ingredients. Mix well and serve.

LANGUAGE GAMES

MR POTATO HEAD
Cut out a large felt potato and a variety of felt facial features. Put the potato on the felt board. Let the children add features to change him from *MR POTATO* to *MR POTATO HEAD*. Take off the features and make a different *MR POTATO HEAD*.
VARIATION:
Cut out 2 felt potatoes. Make one *MR POTATO HEAD*, then make his twin by adding identical features to the second potato.

POTATO SORT
Bring a variety of colors and sizes of real potatoes to circle time. Talk about the similarities and differences. Set 2 plates on the floor. Tell the children that you want them to sort the potatoes by size - large and small. Hold up each potato and have the children call out large or small, then put it on a plate.
VARIATION:
Arrange the potatoes from smallest to largest - mix rearrange them from largest to smallest

ACTIVE GAMES

POTATO SOUP

Make 10 potato necklaces with the numbers from 1 to 10 written on them. Using a clothesline make a big circle to represent the soup pot. Have the children sit around it. Teach the children the *POTATO SOUP* song and then give ten children the necklaces to wear while singing. Now sing the song and as each number is sung, that child should get into the soup pot and jump up and down as if boiling. At the end of the song, the soup is done and everyone can pretend to eat it.

POTATO SOUP

1 little, 2 little, 3 little potatoes,
4 little, 5 little, 6 little potatoes,
7 little, 8 little, 9 little potatoes,
10 little potatoes in the pot.

Boil, boil, boil, bubble
Boil, boil, boil, bubble
Boil, boil, boil, bubble.
Keep boiling 'til the soup is done.
Liz Wilmes

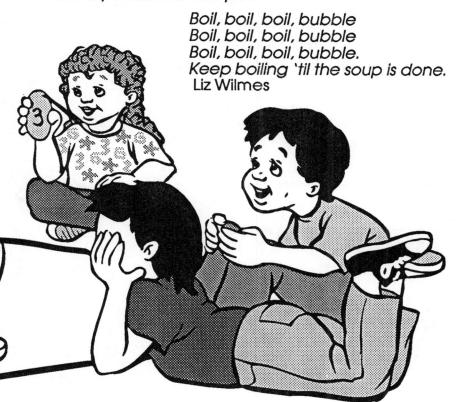

BOOKS

THOMAS BERGER - *THE MOUSE AND THE POTATO*
ANITA LOBEL - *POTATOES, POTATOES*
BARRIE WATT - *POTATO*

FRUITS

MAKE A SIMPLE BOOK ABOUT FRUITS THAT GROW ON TREES, WHICH CHILDREN CAN EASILY `READ.' TO MAKE THE BOOK USE THE TREE PATTERN AND CUT OUT A FRONT AND BACK COVER ALONG WITH 7-10 PAGES. BUY FRUIT STICKERS. PUT ONE TYPE OF FRUIT (ORANGES, LEMONS, GRAPEFRUIT, BANANAS, COCONUT, PEACHES, PINEAPPLE, NECTARINES, PEARS, TANGERINES, APPLES, CHERRIES, ETC.) ON EACH TREE PAGE. WRITE THE NAME OF THE FRUIT ON THE PAGE. PUNCH TWO HOLES IN THE COVERS AND PAGES AND LINK THEM TOGETHER WITH METAL RINGS.

BRING THE BOOK, ALONG WITH PIECES OF REAL FRUIT TO MATCH EACH PAGE, TO CIRCLE TIME. AS YOU READ THE BOOK, HOLD UP THE PIECES OF FRUIT. AFTER YOU'VE READ IT, BEGIN AGAIN. THIS TIME YOU TURN THE PAGES AND LET THE CHILDREN `READ' IT TOGETHER AND IDENTIFY THE FRUITS.

EXTENSION:

PUT IT ON YOUR BOOKSHELF.

Dawn Zavodsky

FINGERPLAYS

BLACKBERRIES

Blackberries, blackberries on the hill.
How many pails can you fill?
Briers are thick and briers scratch.
But we'll pick all the berries
In the blackberry patch.

THE APPLE

Here is an apple (Form fingers in circle.)
Big and round and fat.
Here is the core (Make a fist.)
But you can't eat that.

HOW MANY APPLES

How many apples do you see?
Can you count them? 1, 2, 3.

How many green ones?
How many red?

Now eat an apple
And go to bed.
(Cut green and red felt apples
to use with the rhyme.)

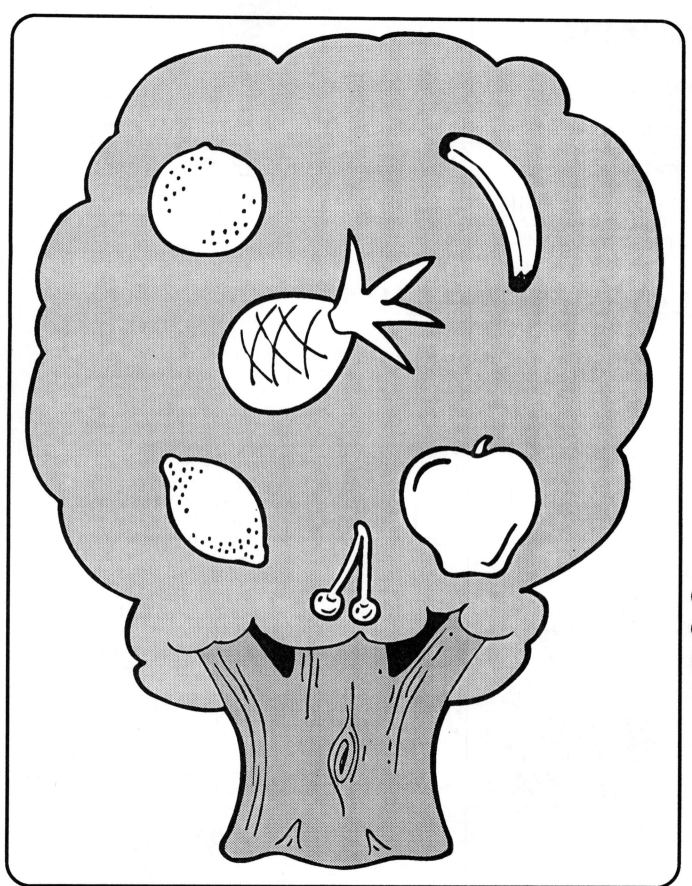

FOODS

SNACK

FRUIT PIZZA
YOU'LL NEED
Refrigerator biscuits
Cream cheese
Sliced fruit

TO MAKE: Flatten the biscuits in a shallow pan to form a crust. Bake at 425° for 8-10 minutes. Cool. Spread the crust with cream cheese. Top the pizza with your favorite fruits.

LANGUAGE GAMES

EXPLORE A FRUIT

Each day choose a fruit and explore it with the children. Pick fruits with different characteristics, colors, and sizes. For example, an apple is round, with white `meat' and a colored skin, has seeds in the middle, a stem, maybe a leaf, and is firm when you squeeze or bite into it. An orange is also round, but its skin and `meat' are the same color, sometimes has seeds, no stem or leaf, and is a little softer when you squeeze or bite into it. Try grapes, watermelon, and maybe blueberries.

If possible, use all five senses as you explore each one. What does each sense tell you about the fruit?

FEEL AND GUESS

Put a variety of fruit in a pillow case. Have a child reach in, feel a fruit, guess what it is, and pull it out. Everyone call out what it is. Set it on a tray. Continue until all of the fruit is out. Touch each fruit and have the children say what it is. Touch again and again going faster, faster, faster!

LANGUAGE GAMES

FRUIT WHISPER

Cut out a variety of fruit pictures from catalogues or magazines. Back them with lightweight cardboard. Hold up each one and have the children quietly say what it is.

Put all of the pictures in the middle of the circle. Call on one child. He should look at the fruit pictures, pick one, and whisper it to a child next to him. That child whispers it to the next child, and so on. After several children have heard it, say to the last child, *"Get the picture of the fruit which (child's name) just whispered to you."* That child goes to the middle and picks up the picture. Everyone looks at it and whispers what it is. The child gives you the picture. Call on another child to pick one of the fruits and whisper it to the child next to him. Continue until all of the fruits have been identified.

FRUIT MATCH

Get matching pictures and real/model fruit. Pass them out. Say *"Who has a picture of an apple? (Child holds it up.) Put it in the middle."* Then say, *"Who has the real/model apple? (Child holds it up.) Put it next to the picture."* Keep matching until all of the pairs are in the middle.

LITTLE JACK HORNER

Teach your children *LITTLE JACK HORNER*. After they know the words, let them take turns naming different fruits for Jack to pull out of his Christmas pie.

LITTLE JACK HORNER
Little Jack Horner sat in a corner
Eating his Christmas pie.
He put in his thumb, and pulled out a plum
And said, "What a good boy am I!"

F
O
O
D
S

ACTIVE GAMES

BOB FOR APPLES

Set a big tub of water on the floor. Put at least one apple for each child in it. (Mix red, yellow, and green apples.) Have 2 or 3 small hand-held food strainers. Have the children stand around the table. Give several children strainers. They should try to catch an apple in their strainers. When they do, everyone clap for them. The child should give his strainer to someone else and put his apple in a basket. Continue until everyone has bobbed for apples.
EXTENSION:
Quarter some of the apples and have them for snack.

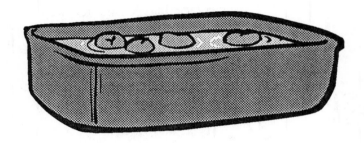

FRUIT HUNT

Get fruit stickers. Cut them into individual sections. Hide them all over the room. Tell the children that you have hidden lots of fruit stickers. When you say "*Fruit Hunt,*" they should look, find one, and come back to the circle time area. When everyone is back, have the children name their fruits and stick them on the backs of their hands. Say "*Fruit Hunt*" again. Let the children look for another sticker. Continue until all of the stickers have been found.

BOOKS

ROBERT McCLOSKEY - *BLUEBERRIES FOR SAL*
EMILY McCULLY - *PICNIC*
ALI MITGUTSCH - *FROM SEED TO PEAR*
DON AND AUDREY WOOD - *THE LITTLE MOUSE, THE RED RIPE STRAWBERRY, AND THE BIG HUNGRY BEAR*

WATERMELON

FOR OPENERS

PUT A WHOLE WATERMELON IN A BAG WHICH HAS HANDLES. COVER THE WATERMELON SO YOU CAN'T SEE WHAT IT IS. BRING THE BAG TO CIRCLE TIME AND PUT IT IN THE MIDDLE OF THE GROUP. TELL THE CHILDREN THAT YOU PUT A FRUIT IN THE BAG AND YOU WANT THEM TO GUESS WHAT IT IS.

HAVE EACH CHILD COME UP AND LIFT THE BAG. IS IT HEAVY OR LIGHT? THEN ASK, *"COULD IT BE AN APPLE? (YES OR NO?) COULD IT BE A BANANA? (YES OR NO? WHY?) COULD IT BE A STRAWBERRY? (YES OR NO? WHY?)* WHAT DO THE CHILDREN THINK IT COULD BE? AFTER GUESSING TAKE THE WATERMELON OUT OF THE BAG. TALK ABOUT TIMES THE CHILDREN HAVE EATEN WATERMELON.

LANGUAGE GAMES

EXPLORE A WATERMELON

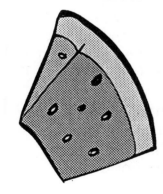

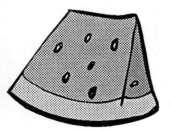

Bring a whole watermelon along with a tray, spoon, and knife (safety) to circle time. Set the watermelon out so that everyone can easily see it. Talk about what it looks like. Turn it over, look again. Have several (all) of the children touch the rhine and then discuss how it feels. Set the watermelon on the tray and cut it open. (Remember safety.) What are the children's first observations? Does the watermelon smell?

Have the children make binoculars with their hands and look at the watermelon even more closely. What else do they see? Using a spoon start to take out all of the visible seeds. Let the children count as you do. Cut a slice of watermelon. Hold it up. Do the children see anything new they want to comment on. Using your knife, cut off the fruit from the rhine. Set the fruit on the tray and pass the piece of rhine around. Let the children comment.
EXTENSION:
Cut up the watermelon for snack.

FOODS

105

LANGUAGE GAMES

COUNT THE SEEDS
Cut a giant slice of watermelon out of red posterboard. Cut 10 black posterboard seeds. Lay the watermelon on the floor. Put the seeds on the slice, one at a time, having the children count them as you do. Take the seeds off, letting the children count again. Continue with a different number of seeds.

TASTE IT
Before circle time cut a watermelon into bite size pieces. Put them in a bowl. Pass the watermelon to the children and have them each take one piece and eat it. How does it taste? Tell them that you are going to pass the watermelon again. This time you want them to suck the melon rather than chew it, and see if they can taste the water. How is it? Pass the melon again. This time let it `melt' in their mouths. How does it feel sitting on their tongues?

WATERMELON WHISPER
Whisper "*watermelon*" over and over. As you repeat it, whisper another fruit once. Stop. Ask the children, "*What other fruit did I whisper?*" They should whisper what it was. Have the children listen again as you whisper "*watermelon........*" this time adding a different fruit. Have children whisper the other fruit. Continue with more series.

ACTIVE GAMES

SEED, SEED, WATERMELON

Have the children form a circle and play *SEED, SEED, WATERMELON*, a variation of *DUCK, DUCK, GOOSE*.

BALANCE THE SEEDS

Divide the children into 2 groups. Lay a clothesline about 10 feet away. Give each child in one group a spoon. Put one seed on each spoon. Have the children balance their seeds as they walk over to the clothesline and back again. Have each child hand his spoon to someone in the second group. Add 1 or 2 more seeds to the spoons and have the children walk over and back. Hand the spoons back to the first group, add more seeds, and continue. Keep going until the spoons are full.

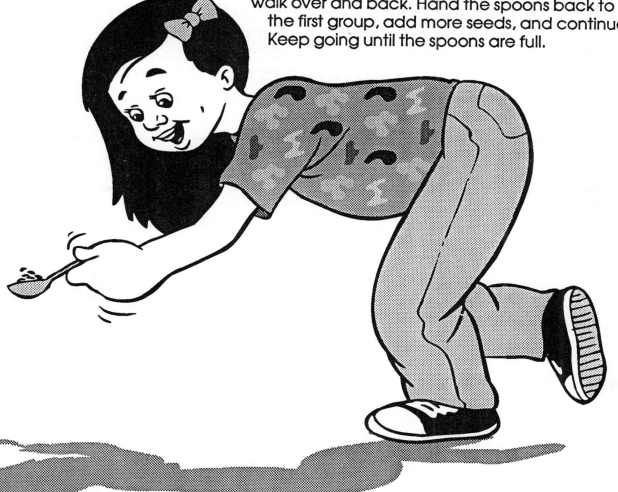

BOOKS

EMILY MCCULLY — *PICNIC*
CYNTHIA RYLANT — *RELATIVES CAME*

BREAD

FOR OPENERS

TAKE A FIELD TRIP TO A LOCAL GROCERY STORE, PREFERABLY ONE THAT HAS ITS OWN BAKERY. ARRANGE THE TRIP AHEAD OF TIME WITH THE MANAGER. HAVE HIM/HER SHOW THE CHILDREN THE BREAD SHELVES. GO SLOWLY AND TALK ABOUT ALL OF THE TYPES OF BREAD. IF TIME ALLOWS GO TO OTHER PARTS OF THE STORE WHICH CONTAIN BREAD, SUCH AS THE COOLERS AND FREEZERS. MAKE THE BAKERY THE LAST STOP. HAVE ONE OF THE BAKERS SHOW THE CHILDREN ROLLS, BREAD, AND OTHER BAKERY GOODS IN VARIOUS STAGES OF PRODUCTION. TAKE TIME TO HAVE A TASTE OF SEVERAL TYPES OF BREADS EITHER AT THE STORE ITSELF OR BACK AT THE CENTER.

FINGERPLAYS

SODA BREAD
Soda bread and soft bread
Crazy bread and hard bread
Loaf bread, cornbread
Plain bread and biscuits.

SNACK

TOAST
YOU'LL NEED
Bagels
Raisin bread
English muffins

TO MAKE: Toast a different type of bread each day. Discuss the similarities and differences.

LANGUAGE GAMES

TASTE TEST

On different days compare a variety of breads. Look at the bread samples and talk about how they are similar and different. Taste them. How are they the same and different? After several days talk about how they compare to the previous breads.

- Rye and white
- Bagels and biscuits
- Banana bread and corn bread
- French bread and sourdough
- Hot dog buns and pita bread

CHOOSE A BREAD

Tell the children a meal that you are going to make and let them choose the breads they could use with it. For example:

- *"I'm going to make a cheese, lettuce, and tomato sandwich. What bread should I use?"*
- *"I'm going to fix spaghetti for my family tonight. What type of bread should I have?"*
- *"I want to have toast with my cereal. What could I have?"*
- *"I'm going to have peanut butter and jelly for a snack. What should I spread them on?"*

(Let children name as many breads as they think would be appropriate.)

THE GIANT SANDWICH

Bring a piece of posterboard and colored markers to circle time. Have the children make a pretend sandwich. Draw a wide brown line near the bottom of the posterboard to represent the bottom piece of bread. Have the children call out what they want on their giant sandwich. As a child names an ingredient, pick a marker and draw a line to represent it. Keep adding more and more ingredients until the children have just the sandwich they'd like. Top it with another piece of bread. `Cut' it up, hand each child a `piece' and `eat' the giant sandwich. Is it good? Is it hard to eat? Are you full? Do you want to make another one?

109

LANGUAGE GAMES

NAME A BREAD   Cut a giant piece of bread from posterboard. Bring it and a marker to circle time. Have the children call out different types of bread. As they do, write the breads down. Hang the list at the children's eye level and add to it as they think of more.
EXTENSION:
Leave space between each type of bread on your list. After circle time, put the giant piece of bread on a table along with several food magazines and glue. Have the children and an adult look for pictures of bread, cut them out, and glue them next to the written word. Now hang up your list.

white   bagel
wheat
rye
toast
french
biscuits
muffins
hamburger buns

BREAD MEMORY   Cut out magazine pictures of 7-8 different breads. Back each one with felt or magnet tape. Bring the pictures and felt/magnet board to circle time. Put all of the pictures on the board. Point to each one and name it. Have the children cover their eyes and take one bread away. Now have the children uncover their eyes, look at the breads, and call out which one is missing. Have the children cover their eyes again and take another bread away, uncover their eyes, look and name the bread which is missing. Repeat until all of the breads are off the board.

ACTIVE GAMES

BAKE BREAD

Make bread/rolls with your children. Buy the prepared dough and follow the directions on the package or make it from scratch.

HOT ROLLS
YOU'LL NEED:
1 pkg dry yeast
1 cup warm water
1/3 cup sugar
1/3 cup liquid oil
3 cups flour
1t salt

TO MAKE: Pour the warm water into a large mixing bowl. Stir in the yeast until dissolved. Add the remaining ingredients and mix well. Flour the table a little and put the dough on it. Knead the dough until it is totally mixed - between 5 and 7 minutes. Add more flour if necessary. Put the dough back into the bowl and let it rise until doubled.

Punch the dough to let the air out and knead for a minute or so. Divide the dough into pieces (as many as you have children). Let them form the balls into rolls and put on a greased cookie sheet. Bake at 450° for 8-10 minutes.

Let cool and serve with a glass of milk.

FOODS

BOOKS

CRESCENT DRAGONWAGON - *THIS IS THE BREAD I BAKED FOR NED*
ANN MORRIS - *BREAD, BREAD, BREAD*

DAIRY

MAKE A SIMPLE SHELF BY FOLDING A PIECE OF WHITE POSTERBOARD IN HALF LENGTHWISE. WRITE *"DAIRY CASE"* ACROSS THE BACKSIDE AND SET IT ON THE TABLE. GET EMPTY DAIRY CARTONS, BOXES AND CONTAINERS. (YOGURT, MILK, EGGS, BUTTER, COTTAGE CHEESE, CHEESE) SET THEM IN YOUR DAIRY CASE. POINT TO EACH ONE, NAME IT, AND TALK ABOUT IT.

   ON ANOTHER PIECE OF POSTERBOARD, MAKE A CHART WITH CHILDREN SHOWING HOW MANY OF THEM EAT EACH PRODUCT. WRITE ALL OF THE DAIRY PRODUCTS DOWN THE LEFT HAND SIDE OF THE BOARD. ACROSS THE TOP WRITE *"YES"* AND *"NO."*

   POINT TO THE FIRST DAIRY PRODUCT AND SAY TO THE CHILDREN, *"THOSE WHO EAT _____ STAND UP. THOSE WHO DO NOT EAT _____ STAY SITTING DOWN."* COUNT THE CHILDREN WHO ARE SITTING AND WRITE THAT NUMBER ON THE CHART UNDER THE `NO' COLUMN. COUNT THOSE WHO ARE STANDING AND WRITE THAT NUMBER ON THE CHART UNDER THE `YES' COLUMN. CONTINUE UNTIL YOU HAVE CHARTED ALL OF THE DAIRY FOODS. WHICH FOODS DO THE CHILDREN EAT MOST/LEAST?

FINGERPLAYS

THIS IS THE WAY WE CHURN THE CREAM
(tune: "Here We Go 'Round the Mulberry Bush")
This is the way we churn the cream,
Churn the cream, churn the cream.
This is the way we churn the cream
To make the creamy butter.

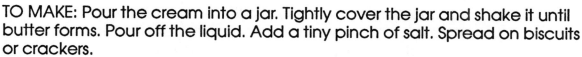

SNACK

HOMEMADE BUTTER
YOU'LL NEED
1 clean small unbreakable jar for each child
1T whipping cream for each child
Pinch salt (optional)

TO MAKE: Pour the cream into a jar. Tightly cover the jar and shake it until butter forms. Pour off the liquid. Add a tiny pinch of salt. Spread on biscuits or crackers.
HINT: A pint of whipping cream equals 32 tablespoons.

LANGUAGE GAMES

FILL THE DAIRY CASE

Bring the dairy case and cartons, containers, and boxes that you used for the *"For Opener"* activity to circle time. Have the products off to the side. Say to the children that the grocer would like them to fill the dairy case. Give the children directions:

- *"John, put the cottage cheese in the middle of the dairy case."*
- *"Tabatha, put the small milk cartons behind the cottage cheese."*
- *"Sammi, put the yogurt on the left side (point) of the case."*
- *"Dick, set the butter between the yogurt and the cottage cheese."*

Continue until all of the products are in the case.

CHEESE, CHEESE

Have the children name all of the different ways they eat cheese - in sandwiches, on crackers, sprinkled on spaghetti, with macaroni, and so on.

FOODS

LANGUAGE GAMES

GO-TOGETHERS Cut out pictures of different foods including lots of dairy products. Back each one with felt or magnet tape. Bring the pictures and felt/magnet board to circle time.

Hold up one picture, name it, and put it on the board. Hold up a second picture. Ask the children, *"Does this one go with* (point to first picture)?*" Why? Why not?"* Put them near each other if they go-together and apart if they do not. (Remember, there are no `right or wrong' answers, just what the children decide.)

WHICH ONE DOESN'T BELONG? Bring dairy food containers and non-dairy food containers to circle time. Show them to the children. Put them in a grocery bag and have the children cover their eyes. Take 4-5 containers out, all but one being for a dairy product. Line them up. Have the children uncover their eyes, look at the food containers, and name the one which doesn't belong. Call on different children to put the containers back into the bag. Cover up again and set out another series of containers. Continue in this manner.

LISTEN CAREFULLY Have the children stand up. Begin naming dairy foods. After you've said several, name a non-dairy food. As soon as they hear the non-dairy food the children should sit down. Have them call out the non-dairy food and then try to remember the dairy foods which you named. After the discussion have the children stand up and play the game again.

114

ACTIVE GAMES

PASS ONE MILK

Get 5 empty cartons of milk. Teach your children the chant *PASS ONE MILK*. Give a child one milk carton, start singing and passing it around the circle. At the beginning of the second verse, give another child a milk carton and continue singing. Add more milk cartons as the chant continues.

> *PASS ONE MILK*
>
> *Pass one milk 'round and 'round*
> *'Round and 'round, 'round and 'round.*
> *Pass one milk 'round and 'round*
> *'Round the circle.*
> *Pass two milks 'round and 'round*
> *Pass three milks.........*
> *Pass four milks.........*
> *Pass five milks........*

SILLY SIMON

Play a simple variation of Simon Says. Give the children directions about dairy products, some of which make sense and some of which do not. If the direction makes sense the children should do it; if it does not, they should call out, *"Silly Simon!"*

- *"Simon says, 'Drink your milk.'"*
- *"Simon says, 'Stir your yogurt.'"*
- *"Simon says, 'Drink your egg.'"*
- *"Simon says, 'Spread your butter.'"*
- Continue

BOOKS

DONALD CARRICK - *MILK*
DR. SEUSS - *GREEN EGGS AND HAM*

FOODS

CEREAL

ABOUT A WEEK BEFORE YOU BEGIN TALKING ABOUT CEREALS, SEND A NOTE HOME TO YOUR PARENTS ASKING THEM TO SAVE THE BOXES FROM THEIR CHILDREN'S FAVORITE CEREALS. HAVE THE CHILDREN BRING THE EMPTY BOXES TO SCHOOL. USING REMOVABLE LABELS WRITE EACH CHILD'S NAME ON HIS BOX. PUT THEM IN ONE PLACE. (HAVE EXTRA CEREAL BOXES AVAILABLE.)

BRING ALL OF THE CEREAL BOXES TO CIRCLE TIME. HOLD UP ONE BOX, READ THE NAME, AND SAY, *"BARBARA LIKES _____."* LET BARBARA NAME THE CEREAL. GIVE THE BOX TO BARBARA. HOLD UP AND IDENTIFY THE OTHER CEREAL BOXES IN THE SAME WAY.

NAME ONE OF THE CEREALS, SUCH AS OATMEAL. HAVE THE CHILDREN WHO BROUGHT OATMEAL BOXES STAND UP. GO AROUND THE GROUP AND NAME THOSE CHILDREN. EVERYONE CLAP. HAVE THEM BRING THEIR OATMEAL BOXES BACK TO THE FRONT. NAME ANOTHER CEREAL AND REPEAT THE ACTIVITY. AFTER ALL OF THE CEREALS ARE BACK, COUNT EACH TYPE AND SEE WHICH ONES ARE YOUR CHILDREN'S FAVORITES. SET UP A DISPLAY OF `FAVORITE CEREALS' ON A SPECIAL SHELF OR TABLE.

SNACK

CEREAL MIX
YOU'LL NEED
Different cereals

TO MAKE: Let the children put handfuls of different cereals into a large bowl. Mix. Scoop the mixture into individual bowls and have plain or with a little milk.

LANGUAGE GAMES

CEREAL PUZZLES

Collect 10 or more different cereal boxes with which the children are familiar. Cut off the front sides. Cut each side into two pieces using a different type of cut, such as wavy, pointed, straight, circular, jagged, etc.

Pass out the puzzle pieces to the children. Say, *"I'm looking for the `Cheerios' puzzle. If you have a `Cheerios' piece bring it up."* Match the 2 Cheerios pieces on the floor. Repeat with all of the puzzles. After they have been put together, hold each one up and have the children call out what cereal it is.

`YEAH' FOR CEREAL

Line up various cereal boxes for the children to see. Point to each one and have the children call out its name. Go back to the first one. Have a child come up and hold it. Whoever likes that cereal calls out *"Yeah"* and claps. Whoever doesn't like the cereal is quiet. Continue with the remaining cereals.

WHAT'S IN THE BOX?

Get various unopened boxes of cereal. Put them in a grocery bag so no one can see them. Pull one out. Ask the children what cereal they think is in the box. How do they know? What does the cereal actually look like? Open the box and give each child a little to taste. Do they like it? Continue talking about and tasting the other cereals.

FOODS

117

LANGUAGE GAMES

SNAP, CRACKLE, AND POP

Have the children pretend that they are `Rice Krispies' cereal. Divide the children into 3 groups - *snap, crackle,* and *pop.* The children who are `snap' can snap their fingers, the children who are `crackle' can slap their thighs, and the children who are `pop' can pop their cheeks. Practice the noises. Designate a space in the middle of the area to be your bowl.

Now you're ready to shake the cereal into the bowl. Quietly chant, "*Shake, shake, shake....*" as the children scoot into the bowl. After all of the `cereal' is in the bowl, slowly pour the milk over each kernel of cereal. As you do, that kernel begins to make his noise. Soon the whole bowl is *snapping, crackling,* and *popping.*

Start eating your cereal. The noises get quieter and quieter as the `cereal' slowly scoots out of the bowl. Soon you've eaten all of the `Rice Krispies' and nothing is left in the bowl.

EXTENSION:
Have Rice Krispies and milk for snack.

ACTIVE GAMES

WE EAT CEREAL

Get 4-5 types of cereals which are shaped like circles and squares. (`Cheerios, Chex, Shredded Wheat, Kix,'` etc.) Lay about 10 pieces of each on a tray. Put the tray in the middle. Teach your children the song, *WE EAT CEREAL*. Have the children start singing and walk around the tray. When they've finished singing they should freeze. Call on 5-6 children to walk to the tray, pick up and eat a certain shaped cereal. Sing and play again. Continue until all of the cereal has been eaten.

VARIATION:

Change the third line to ABCs, ABCs. Put `Alpha Bits'` cereal on the tray and let the children pick out certain letters.

WE EAT CEREAL
(tune: Frere Jacques)
We eat cereal, we eat cereal
Yes we do, yes we do.
Circles and squares, circles and squares
We know them all, we know them all.
  Liz Wilmes

119

PIZZA

MAKE A FELT PIZZA WITH THE CHILDREN. (THIS WILL BE A 2-DAY ACTIVITY.)

DAY 1—BRING AN EMPTY PIZZA BOARD TO CIRCLE TIME. (COULD CUT A LARGE ROUND POSTERBOARD CIRCLE.) SAY TO THE CHILDREN, *"LET'S PRETEND THAT WE ARE GOING TO MAKE A PIZZA. WHAT SHOULD WE PUT ON IT?"* LET THE CHILDREN NAME ALL OF THE INGREDIENTS THAT THEY WOULD LIKE ON THEIR PIZZA. WRITE DOWN WHAT THEY WANT.

USING APPROPRIATE COLORS OF FELT, CUT OUT PIECES TO REPRESENT THE VARIOUS INGREDIENTS ALONG WITH ROUND PIECES OF BEIGE FELT FOR THE CRUST AND RED FELT FOR THE TOMATO SAUCE.

DAY 2—BRING THE PIZZA BOARD AND THE FELT PIECES TO CIRCLE TIME. SHOW THEM TO THE CHILDREN AND NAME EACH ONE. BEGIN TO MAKE THE PIZZA BY PUTTING THE CRUST AND TOMATO SAUCE ON THE CARDBOARD. ASK WHAT INGREDIENT THE CHILDREN WOULD LIKE TO PUT ON FIRST. LET THE CHILDREN PUT THE PIECES ON. KEEP ADDING THE DIFFERENT TOPPINGS UNTIL THE PIZZA IS FINISHED.

PUT YOUR PIZZA IN THE OVEN TO BAKE. WHILE IT IS BAKING, TALK WITH THE CHILDREN ABOUT REAL PIZZA THEY HAVE EATEN. WHEN FINISHED `EAT` YOUR PIZZA.

EXTENSION:
PUT THE PIZZA BOARD AND PIECES ON A TABLE FOR CHILDREN TO CREATE THEIR OWN PIZZAS DURING FREE CHOICE.

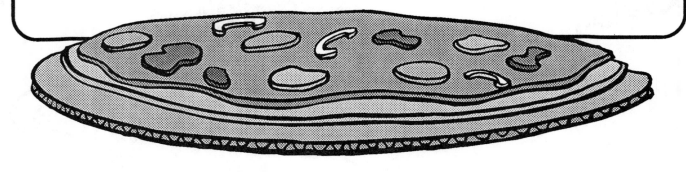

SNACK

EASY PIZZAS
YOU'LL NEED
English muffins
Pizza sauce
Shredded cheese
Ripe olives, pitted

TO MAKE: Spread pizza sauce on the muffin halves and sprinkle cheese over the sauce. Top with sliced olives. Toast in the broiler until the cheese is melted.

LANGUAGE GAMES

WE LIKE PIZZA Make a chart of different pizza ingredients and record who likes each one. Leave room at the bottom to add more ingredients.

olives					DJ
mushrooms	Liz			Eric	
sausage	Liz	Greg	Dick	Eric	DJ
peppers	Liz	Greg		Eric	DJ
onions			Dick	Eric	DJ

FOODS

LANGUAGE GAMES

CRAZY PIZZA

Bring your color wheel and an empty pizza board to circle time. Put the pizza board on the floor. Tell the children that they are going to make a crazy pizza with all types of foods on it. Have a child flick the spinner on the color wheel and name the color it points to. Let a child name a food to put on the pizza that is the same color. Flick the spinner again and name another food. Have all of the children call out the two foods on the crazy pizza so far. Flick again, add a third ingredient, and name all 3 foods. Continue adding more and more ingredients until the pizza is full. Pretend to eat your crazy pizza. How do you like it?

SMALL, MEDIUM, OR LARGE?

Make 3 different size round pizzas. To make them, cut out 9", 12", and 16" circles from posterboard. Using colored markers draw the ingredients on each one. Cut each one into 4 equal slices.

Bring the slices to circle time. Hold up one of each size and have the children decide which one is the small, medium, and large slice. Then put the 3 slices on the floor for everyone to see. Mix up the remaining slices and put them in a bag. Have each of the children pick a piece out of the bag and look at it. Ask, *"Who has a pizza slice for the small pizza?"* (Have the children put their pizza together.) Repeat for the medium and large pizzas. After the pizzas are put together, ask the children which size their family would buy.
EXTENSION:
Put the pizzas near the other puzzles for the children to work during free choice.

ACTIVE GAMES

EXTRA-EXTRA LARGE, PLEASE

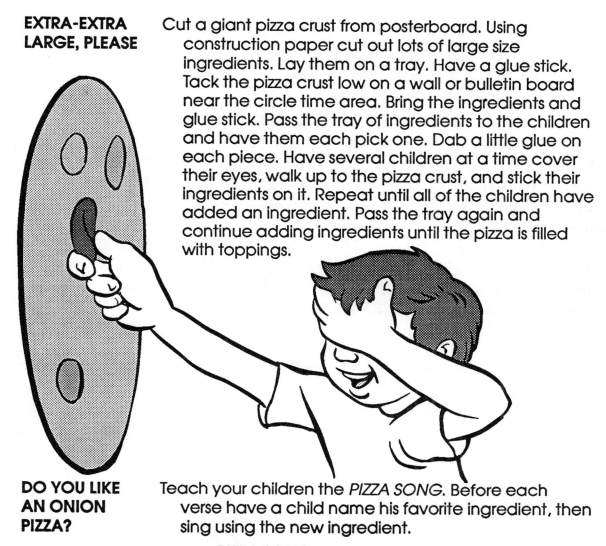

Cut a giant pizza crust from posterboard. Using construction paper cut out lots of large size ingredients. Lay them on a tray. Have a glue stick. Tack the pizza crust low on a wall or bulletin board near the circle time area. Bring the ingredients and glue stick. Pass the tray of ingredients to the children and have them each pick one. Dab a little glue on each piece. Have several children at a time cover their eyes, walk up to the pizza crust, and stick their ingredients on it. Repeat until all of the children have added an ingredient. Pass the tray again and continue adding ingredients until the pizza is filled with toppings.

DO YOU LIKE AN ONION PIZZA?

Teach your children the *PIZZA SONG*. Before each verse have a child name his favorite ingredient, then sing using the new ingredient.

PIZZA SONG
(tune: Do You Know the Muffin Man?)

Do you like an onion pizza,
An onion pizza, an onion pizza?
Do you like an onion pizza?
Eat it if you do! (Pretend to eat.)

Continue with the children's favorite toppings.

BOOKS

KAREN BARBOUR - *LITTLE NINO'S PIZZERIA*
MARGARET REY - *CURIOUS GEORGE AND THE PIZZA*

FOODS

LEAVES

MAKE A SIMPLE STRIP-TYPE SEQUENCE CHART SHOWING HOW A LEAF GROWS. TO MAKE THE CHART CUT A GIANT LEAF OUT OF POSTERBOARD. IN THE MIDDLE OF THE LEAF CUT TWO 2" WIDE SLITS ABOUT TWO INCHES APART. CUT A 2" BY 15" STRIP OF POSTERBOARD. ON THE STRIP DRAW SIMPLE PICTURES SHOWING HOW A LEAF DEVELOPS. SLIP IT THROUGH THE TWO SLITS.

   BRING THE LEAF TO CIRCLE TIME. SHOW THE CHILDREN THE FIRST PICTURE ON THE STRIP. TELL THEM ABOUT IT. PULL THE STRIP SO THAT THE SECOND PICTURE SHOWS. TELL THEM ABOUT IT. CONTINUE SHOWING THE CHILDREN THE PICTURES OF THE DEVELOPING LEAF AND TELLING THEM ABOUT IT.

FINGERPLAYS

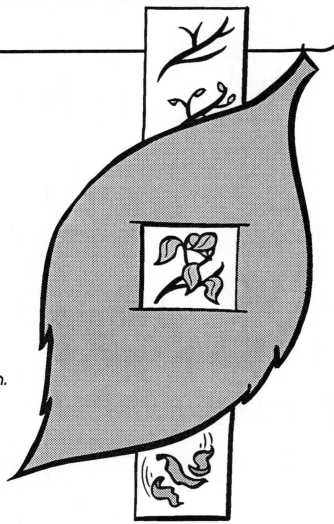

AUTUMN

Leaves are floating softly down.
They make a carpet on the ground.
Then swish, the wind comes whistling by,
And sends them dancing to the sky.

GENTLY FALLING LEAVES

Little leaves fall gently down,
Red and yellow, orange and brown.

Whirling, whirling 'round and 'round,
Quietly without a sound.

Falling softly to the ground,
Down - and down - and down - and down.

LITTLE LEAVES

The little leaves are falling down,
'Round and 'round, 'round and 'round.
The little leaves are falling down,
Falling to the ground.

LEAVES GROW

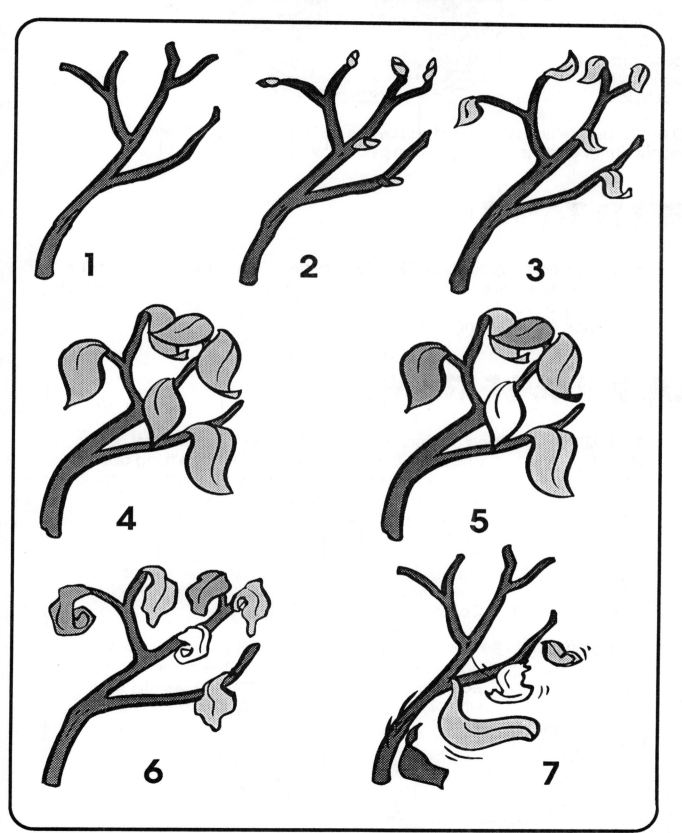

1

2

3

4

5

6

7

SNACK

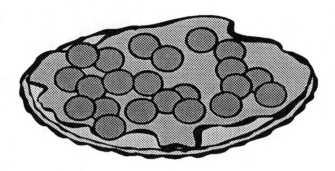

LEAFY TREES
YOU'LL NEED
Round crackers
Peanut butter
Frozen peas

TO MAKE: Let the children make trees by spreading their crackers with peanut butter and then adding frozen pea 'leaves.'

FIELD TRIPS

● Take different types of *LEAF WALKS* with the children. They could look for different size leaves, such as one day look only for giant leaves and another day tiny leaves. Put them on trays with magnifying glasses so that the children can examine them more carefully.

LANGUAGE GAMES

EXPLORING LEAVES
Bring 6-7 very different real leaves to circle time. Hold one up so everyone can see it. Tell one thing about the leaf. Pass it to the child next to you, have him look at it, and tell one more thing about it. He should give the leaf to another child who tells something about it. Continue passing the leaf around. As the children are examining the leaf encourage them to use all appropriate senses - How does it feel? Does it smell? Does it make any noise? Can you eat leaves? Etc.

LEAF COUNT
Bring 4-5 twigs with leaves still on them to circle time. Have a child hold up one of the twigs. You touch each leaf on the twig as the children count. Repeat with all of the twigs. Which twig has the most leaves? Least?

LANGUAGE GAMES

LOOK CAREFULLY

Gather about 10 distinct leaves. Lay them on a piece of posterboard. Carefully trace their outlines. Put the leaves in a basket.

Lay the game board on the floor. Have a child pull one leaf out of the basket and match it to the outline on the board. Repeat until all of the leaves have been matched.

Describe one of the leaves, such as *"I am looking for a large gold and red leaf. Who sees it?"* Have a child take it off of the board and put it back into the basket. Continue until all of the leaves are back in the basket.
EXTENSION:
Put the game on a table for children to play during free choice.

PASS THE LEAVES

Back 6-7 real or construction paper leaves ranging in size from small to huge with felt or magnet tape.
Bring the leaves and the felt/magnet board to circle time.

Give one leaf to a child. Have him begin passing it around the circle. As the children pass the leaf everyone chant, *"Pass, pass, pass...."* After the leaf has passed by several children, you say, *"Stop."* The child holding the leaf puts it on the felt/magnet board. Repeat with the rest of the leaves.

After all of the leaves are on the board, let the children put them in order from small to huge - huge to small.

FALLING LEAVES   Cut all colors and sizes of a specific leaf. Using clothespins,

clip them to an empty branch. Set a basket nearby. Have the children look at all of the leaves. Say, *"The large red leaf is falling off of the branch. Sami, put it in the basket."* That child unclips the leaf and lets it float into the basket. Continue until all of the leaves are off of the branch.

SCIENCE

127

ACTIVE GAMES

LEAF SEARCH

Get 5 boxes or tubs. Cut out a red, orange, yellow, green, and brown construction paper leaf and glue one to each box.

Bring the boxes outside and set them on the ground. Name a color, have the children search for a leaf the color you named, and drop it in the matching box. Name another color and let the children play *LEAF SEARCH* again. Continue until there are leaves in each box.

Bring the boxes back the classroom, count the leaves in each one, and write the numeral on the construction paper leaf.

LEAVES ARE FALLING DOWN

Get red, yellow, orange, and green adhesive dots. (Could use washable markers instead.) Let each child choose a color and put the dot on the back of his hand. Pretend these are leaves. Sing the song and have the children flutter to the ground when their color is sung.

FLUTTERING LEAVES
(tune: Farmer In the Dell)

The leaves are fluttering down
The leaves are fluttering down
Red and yellow, orange and green
The leaves are fluttering down.

BOOKS

CHRIS ARVETIS — *WHY DO LEAVES CHANGE COLOR*
FULVIO TESTA — *LEAVES*
HILDE HOFFMAN (illus.) — *THE GREEN GRASS GROWS ALL AROUND*
JANICE UDRY — *A TREE IS NICE*
CINDY WHEELER — *MARMALADE'S YELLOW LEAF*

FLOWERS

READ THE BOOK *THE TINY SEED* BY ERIC CARLE TO THE CHILDREN. READ IT AGAIN, ONLY THIS TIME USE FELT PIECES TO ENHANCE THE STORY AS YOU READ.

FOR SNACK THIS DAY SERVE SUNFLOWER SEEDS ALONG WITH GRAPE OR APPLE JUICE.

FINGERPLAYS

THE FLOWER

Here's a green leaf,
And here's a green leaf;
That, you see, makes two.

Here is a bud
That makes a flower;
Watch it bloom for you!

MY FLOWER BED

See the blue and yellow blossoms
In the flower bed.
The daisy spreads its petals wide
The tulip bows its head.

RELAXING FLOWERS

Five little flowers
Standing in the sun;
See their heads nodding,
Bowing, one by one.

Down, down, down
Falls the gentle rain,
And the five little flowers
Lift up their heads again!

SCIENCE

FINGERPLAYS

GROW A LITTLE ROSE

Dig a little hole.
Plant a little seed.
Pour a little water.
Pull a little weed.

Chase a little bug -
Heigh-ho, there he goes!
Give a little sunshine,
Grow a little rose.

PITTER PATTER

Pitter, patter falls the rain,
On the roof and window pane.

Softly, softly it comes down,
Makes a stream that runs around.

Flowers lift their heads and say:
"A nice cool drink for us today."

FIELD TRIPS

- Arrange a trip to a local florist. Ask the florist to show the children how the flowers are delivered, where they are stored, and what flower arrangers do with the different flowers.

- Walk around your neighborhood and look for blooming flowers. Are there flowers around homes, in the park, in flower boxes, or hanging from planters?

CLASSROOM VISITORS

- Ask a parent who enjoys working with flowers to visit the children and talk with them about how to plant flowers and then care for them. Take the opportunity to plant seeds in individual cups or in several large planters. Take photographs of the flowers every 2-3 days. After being developed, let the children put the photographs in the proper sequence and then into a classroom book.

- Plant a second garden, but put it in a shady area. Compare the two.

130

LANGUAGE GAMES

FLOWER VASE

Make 10-15 pairs of wallpaper flowers. To make each pair, cut a piece of wallpaper into 2 large identical flower shapes. Glue the flowers to paint stir sticks. Make additional pairs by using different wallpaper patterns and/or different flower shapes.

Bring an empty vase and the flowers to circle time. Divide the children into 2 equal groups. Give each child in the first group one of the flowers from each pair. Give the children in the other group the mates. Put the vase where everyone can see it. Have a child from the first group hold up his flower. Everyone in the second group looks at his flower. The child who has the mate joins the first child and they walk over to the vase and put their flowers in it. Now ask a child from the second group to hold up his flower and the children in group one look at theirs. The mates walk to the vase and put their flowers in. Continue until all of the flowers have been paired and put in the vase.

SCIENCE

LANGUAGE GAMES

FLOWER BOX   Several days before this activity let children make
artificial flowers in the art area by cutting
construction paper flowers and gluing them to
popsicle stick stems.

Get a flower box, cardboard box, or wagon. Fill it
with sand. Bring the flower box and flowers to circle
time. Hold 4-5 flowers in your hand. Say to a child,
"Nikki, plant a small red flower in our flower box." The
child comes up, takes the red flower and sticks it in
the sand. Continue until all of the flowers have been
planted.

Set the flower box on a ledge, table, or floor where
the children can easily plant and replant the flowers
during free choice.

FLOWERS GROW   Put magnet tape on the back of the photographs
which you took of your flower garden. (See
Classroom Visitors.) Bring the photos and magnet
board to circle time. Put them on the magnet board
in proper sequence. Talk about how flowers grow.
Now mix up the photographs. Have the children put
them in order again.

**FLOWERS
EVERYWHERE**   Encourage the children to look for flowers as each of
them comes and goes from school. Talk about all of
the places they saw flowers growing.

**I SEE A RED
FLOWER**   Get a flower catalogue. Open it to any pictured
page, hold it so that the children can see it, and
say, *"I see a red flower."* Have a child walk up and
point to one. Continue naming different colors of
flowers on that page and others.
EXTENSION:
Put the catalogue on the book shelf or in the
science area.

ACTIVE GAMES

RING AROUND THE ROSIE

Teach your children this traditional song along with the circle game.

> ### RING AROUND THE ROSIE
> *Ring around the rosie*   (Hold hands and walk in a
> *Pocketful of posies*   circle.)
> *Ashes, ashes*
> *We all fall down.*   (Fall to the floor.)

MUSICAL FLOWERS

Bring a bag full of plastic flowers to circle time. Have the children sit in a circle. Put a vase in the middle. Begin playing music and have the children pass the bag around. Stop the music. The child holding the bag opens it and chooses a flower. He gets up, gives you his flower, and sits back down. Start the music again and continue playing until you are holding a bouquet of flowers. Put the bouquet in a vase and set it on a table or low shelf.

PLANT A GARDEN

Choose several types of flowers which grow well in your area and plant a classroom flower garden with the children. Remember to water, weed, and care for it

BOOKS

ERIC CARLE — *THE TINY SEED*
DEMI — *THE EMPTY POT*
LOIS ELHERT — *PLANTING A RAINBOW*
HELLER RUTH — *A REASON FOR A FLOWER*

S
C
I
E
N
C
E

SEASONS

FOR OPENERS

CLAP AS YOU SING THE FOUR SEASONS SONG.

FOUR SEASONS
(TUNE: SKIP TO MY LOU)

SPRING, SUMMER, FALL, AND WINTER.
SPRING, SUMMER, FALL, AND WINTER.
SPRING, SUMMER, FALL, AND WINTER.
THESE ARE THE FOUR SEASONS.
   LIZ WILMES

FINGERPLAYS

BIG HILL

Here's a great big hill
With snow all over the side.
Let's take our sleds
And down the hill we'll slide.

FALLING RAINDROPS

Raindrops, raindrops!
Falling all around.
Pitter-patter on the rooftops,
Pitter-patter on the ground.

Here is my umbrella.
It will keep me dry.
When I go walking in the rain
I hold it up so high.

DRESS FOR WINTER WEATHER

Let's put on our mittens
And button up our coat.
Wrap a scarf snugly
Around our throat.

Pull on our boots,
Fasten the straps,
And tie on tightly
Our warm winter caps.

Then open the door...
And out we go
Into the soft and feathery snow.

FINGERPLAYS

A LITTLE GIRL'S/BOY'S WALK

A little girl/boy went walking
On a lovely summer day.
S/he say a little rabbit
That quickly ran away.

S/he saw a shining river
Go winding in and out.
And little fishes in it
Were swimming all about.

HAPPY CHILDREN
(tune: Did You Ever See A Lassie)

Happy children in the Springtime,
The Springtime, the Springtime.
Happy children in the Springtime,
Sway this way and that.

WINTER WEATHER

Thumbs in the thumb place,
Fingers all together,
This is the song we sing
In winter weather.

Doesn't matter whether
They're made of wool or leather.

Thumbs in the thumb place,
Fingers all together.
This is the song we sing
In winter weather.

SNACK

Pretend that it is different seasons as you enjoy different drinks:
- SUMMER — Lemonade (Talk about other cooling drinks.)
- FALL — Apple cider (Talk about apples.)
- WINTER — Hot chocolate (Talk about other warm drinks.)
- SPRING — Tomato juice (Talk about planting gardens.)

LANGUAGE GAMES

TALK ABOUT Talk with the children about how they feel, what they like and do not like and what they do during different types of weather. Ask questions such as:
- How do you feel on a rainy day?
- Are you afraid during a certain type of weather?
- What do you like to play when it is hot outside?
- What does it feel like on a windy day?

WHAT'S THE WEATHER? Bring a variety of clothes to circle time which a child might wear in different types of weather. Hold one up and ask, "*I'm going to wear these boots today. What kind of weather is it? (Discuss) What else should I wear?*" (Discuss)

SUMMER-WINTER Play *SUMMER-WINTER*. To play, say something about summer or winter such as, "*We build snowmen in the _____.*" Have the children complete the sentence by shivering if it is winter or sweating if it is summer. Continue with different sentences about the seasons.
- "*It is cold in the _____.*"
- "*We wear shorts in the _____.*"
- "*The trees are bare in the _____.*"
- "*We have picnics in the _____.*"
- Continue

STAY COOL In the summer it is very hot and people try to stay cool. Talk about ways the children do this. In the winter it is very cold and people try to stay warm. Talk about ways children do this.

136

LANGUAGE GAMES

IMAGINATION STRETCHER

Cut a giant wind, snowflake, raindrop, and sun out of colored posterboard. Bring one of them and a marker to circle time each day.

Hold up the weather symbol, such as the snowflake. Ask the children, *"When you think of a snowflake what do you think about?"* Write all of their thoughts on the snowflake. Hang it at their eye level and add to it as the children have more ideas. Continue listing their ideas, and then hanging each weather symbol on different days.

SCIENCE

ACTIVE GAMES

RAKE THE LEAVES

Teach your children this song. As you're singing, do appropriate actions.

RAKE THE LEAVES
(tune: Here We Go 'Round the Mulberry Bush)

*We swim at the beach in summer time
In summertime, in summertime.
We swim at the beach in summertime
Hi-ho, hi-ho, hi-ho.*

We rake leaves in fall time....

We build snowpals in winter time....

We splash puddles in spring time....
    Liz Wilmes

BOOKS

FRANKLYN BRANLEY — *SUNSHINE MAKES SEASONS*
AILEEN FISHER — *I LIKE WEATHER*
GAIL GIBBONS — *THE SEASONS OF ARNOLD'S APPLE TREE*
SHIRLEY HUGHES — *OUT AND ABOUT*
SUSAN PEARSON — *MY FAVORITE TIME OF THE YEAR*
ANNE ROCKWELL — *FIRST COMES SPRING*

RAIN/SNOW

RAIN AND SNOW ARE FORMS OF WATER WHICH FALL FROM CLOUDS IN THE SKY. RAIN IS LIQUID AND SNOW IS MORE SOLID. AS SNOW MELTS IT BECOMES A LIQUID JUST LIKE RAIN.

BEFORE IT RAINS, PUT A CLEAR DISH OUTSIDE. LET IT RAIN AND THEN BRING THE DISH INSIDE. TALK ABOUT WHAT CHILDREN DO WHEN IT RAINS. ON THE NEXT DAY BRING A BAG OF SHAVED ICE TO CIRCLE TIME. POUR IT INTO ANOTHER CLEAR DISH. TALK ABOUT HOW IT LOOKS AND FEELS. PUT THE DISH NEXT TO YOU AND READ THE BOOK `A SNOWY DAY' BY EZRA JACK KEATS. TALK WITH THE CHILDREN ABOUT WHAT THEY DO WHEN IT SNOWS. NOW LOOK AT YOUR DISH OF `SNOW' AND SEE HOW IT HAS CHANGED. COMPARE IT TO YOUR DISH OF RAIN.

EXTENSION:
USE YOUR RAIN AND SNOW WATER FOR WATERCOLOR PAINTING IN THE ART AREA.

FINGERPLAYS

LITTLE RAINDROPS

This is the sun, high up in the sky.
A dark cloud suddenly comes
   sailing by.
These are the raindrops,
Pitter, pattering down.
Watering the flowers
Growing on the ground.

RAINY DAY FUN

Slip on your raincoat.
Pull up your galoshes.
Wade in the puddles.
Make splishes and sploshes.

SNOW

Snow on my forehead
Snow on my knee
Snow on my glasses
Getting hard to see.

Snow on my boots
Snow in my hair
Snow on my mittens
Snow everywhere
   Dick Wilmes

SLEDDING

Here's a great big hill,
With snow all over the side.
Let's pull our sleds up to the top
And down the hill we'll slide.

SCIENCE

SNACK

SNOWFLAKE FRUIT
YOU'LL NEED
Fruit, such as apples, oranges, grapes
Coconut flakes

TO MAKE: Clean and cut the fruit into bite size pieces. Put it in a large bowl and stir it well. Pour coconut into a small dish. Let the children help themselves to the fruit and then pretend that it is snowing by sprinkling coconut flakes on top.

FIELD TRIPS

- After a gentle rain go outside and walk around the neighborhood. Look for places where rain has settled in holes, on leaves, near curbs, etc.

- After a snowfall go outside and walk around the neighborhood. Look for places where snow has collected and formed mounds — near buildings or up against cars. Maybe snowplows have pushed the snow off of the streets onto the curbs.
    If it warms up enough for the snow to melt, take another walk and look for puddles of water.

LANGUAGE GAMES

LET IT SNOW

Cut 10 or more snowflakes out of white construction paper. Back each flake with felt or magnet tape.
    Bring the snowflakes and felt/magnet board to circle time. Let it snow into the classroom by putting a certain number of snowflakes on your board. Have the children count them as you do. How many snowflakes fell? Take the snowflakes off of the board and let it snow again with a different number of flakes. Enjoy counting again and again.
VARIATION:
Play *LET IT RAIN* using raindrops instead of snowflakes.

LANGUAGE GAMES

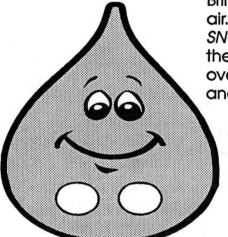

IMAGINATION STRETCHER

Make a raindrop and snowflake finger puppet. Put one on each hand. Put them behind your back. Bring one out and make it float gently through the air. As it floats down say the *RAINDROP OR SNOWFLAKE* sentence. Let a child fill in the blank. Put the raindrop or snowflake behind your back. Repeat over and over thinking of different places that drops and flakes land.

> *"RAINDROP, RAINDROP*
> *FALL GENTLY ON THE _____."*
>
> *"SNOWFLAKE, SNOWFLAKE*
> *FALL GENTLY ON THE _____."*

LISTEN CAREFULLY

Begin saying words all of which are related to snow. After saying several, say a `non' snow word. When the children hear the word which doesn't belong to snow they should clap. Have a child say which word didn't relate. Play over and over using different series of words.

Snow Words	Rain Words
snowman	warm
snowfall	drizzle
slush	showers
snowball	thunderstorm
cold	puddles
blizzard	muddy
icy	lightening
sleet	dark
slippery	
igloo	
snow	
shovel	

WHAT SHOULD I WEAR?

Say to the children, *"It's raining, what should I wear?"* Call on a child to name one thing. Say *"It's snowing, what should I wear?"* Have a child say something to wear. Keep saying either that it is raining or snowing and have children name different pieces of clothing each time.

ACTIVE GAMES

IT'S RAINING, IT'S POURING

Sing this traditional rainy day song with the children, substituting each of their names in the second line. When a child is named he begins snoring and then lies down on the floor. Continue singing until all of the children are 'sleeping.'

IT'S RAINING, IT'S POURING

It's raining, it's pouring
Little (child's name) is snoring
S/he went to bed
And bumped his/her head
And couldn't get up in the morning.

PUDDLE JUMPING

Using posterboard or construction paper, cut big 'puddles' for each child. Have the children stand in a large circle, give each child a puddle and have him set it on the floor in front of him. Give the children directions in relation to the puddles.

- "Hold hands and walk around all of the puddles. Sing the *IT'S RAINING, IT'S POURING* song as you walk. Stop."
- "Hop around your puddle."
- Point in one direction and then say "Take a giant step and move to the puddle next to you."
- "Jump over your new puddle."
- Continue

BOOKS

EZRA JACK KEATS — *THE SNOWY DAY*
BILL MARTIN — *LISTEN TO THE RAIN*
ANNE AND HARLOW ROCKWELL — *THE FIRST SNOWFALL*
URSEL SCHEFFLER — *A WALK IN THE RAIN*
KIYOSHI SOYA — *A HOUSE OF LEAVES*
PETER SPIER — *RAIN*
CHARLOTTE ZOLOTOW — *SOMETHING IS GOING TO HAPPEN*

SHADOWS

FOR OPENERS

GET A LONG, RECTANGULAR WOODEN BLOCK. SHOW IT TO THE CHILDREN. SET IT ON A LARGE PIECE OF WHITE PAPER IN A SUNNY AREA. FIND THE SHADOW AND TRACE AROUND IT WITH A WIDE MARKER. ABOUT A HALF AN HOUR TO AN HOUR LATER GATHER THE CHILDREN AGAIN AND CHECK YOUR BLOCK. NOW WHERE IS THE SHADOW? TRACE AROUND IT AGAIN AND WRITE THE NUMERAL `2' IN THE SHADOW. CONTINUE TO CHECK THE SHADOW, TRACE AROUND IT, AND NUMBER IT.

TALK WITH THE CHILDREN ABOUT WHY THE SHADOW CHANGES EVEN THOUGH THE BLOCK NEVER DOES.

FINGERPLAYS

ME AND MY SHADOW

We're best friends,
My shadow and me.
Wherever I go,
My shadow will be.
　Vohny Moehling

DANCING FINGERS

1 little, 2 little, 3 little shadows (Hold fingers up as you sing.)
4 little, 5 little, 6 little shadows
7 little, 8 little, 9 little shadows
Dancing all around. (Dance your fingers.)

9 little, 8 little, 7 little shadows (Tuck fingers into fist.)
6 little, 5, little, 4 little shadows
3 little, 2, little, 1 little shadow
Resting quietly.

SHADOW WALK

I'm taking my shadow for a walk,
We'll be very quiet, he doesn't talk.
With the sun overhead and the sidewalk below,
We'll walk very fast or tiptoe really slow.
　Vohny Moehling

143

SNACK

SHADOW SANDWICHES
YOU'LL NEED
Dark rye bread
Spreadable toppings
All types of cookie cutters

TO MAKE: Using the cookie cutters, let the children make the shadows by cutting the bread into lots of different shapes and then spreading them with the various toppings. As you eat snack talk about the different shadows which you made.

FIELD TRIPS

- On a sunny day, take a walk around your neighborhood. As you go, look for shadows. Each time you see one, find the real object which is making the shadow. Maybe children would like to make their own shadows on the sidewalk.

LANGUAGE GAMES

**SHADOW
SHAPES**

Before circle time make a construction paper circle, triangle, square and rectangle. Attach a tongue depressor to the side of each one for a handle. Shine a light on a blank wall. Have the children cover their eyes. Make a shadow on the blank wall with one of the shapes. Let the children look at the shadow and call our what shape it is. Repeat the activity with each shape.

Now take one of the shapes and move it closer to the wall. Ask the children what shape it is. Move the shape even closer. Ask the children, *"Did the _____ get larger or smaller?"* (Answer) Move the shape several more times and let the children decide if it is getting larger or smaller.

EXTENSION:
Play `SHADOW SHAPES` again using slightly more detailed shapes like a heart, snow person, kite, moon, etc. Once the children are more comfortable identifying shapes, use even more complicated shapes such as different animals. (See Section 3 for animal shapes.)

144

LANGUAGE GAMES

SHADOW MEMORY
Using black construction paper cut out 6-7 recognizable shadows. Back each one with felt/magnet tape. Bring your felt/magnet board and shadows to circle time.

Put all of the shadows in a row on your board. Point to each one and name it. Have the children cover their eyes and take one shadow away. Have them uncover their eyes, look at the shadows, and call out which one is missing. Repeat the activity until all of the shadows are off of the board.

HOW MANY FINGERS?
Shine a light on a wall. Hold up several fingers. Count them with the children. Make a fist. Hold up a different amount of fingers and count again. After you've done this several times. let a child hold up his fingers and everyone count. Switch children and count again and again.

ACTIVE GAMES

SHADOW PALS
Have the children pair off for a special shadow walk. When you get outside have the children find their shadows on the sidewalk. Then say, "Partners, move your legs so that your shadow legs touch but not your real ones." Continue with other body parts.
- Shadow hands shake.
- Shadow feet step on each other.
- Shadow elbows poke each other.
- Shadow heads knock into each other.
- Continue.

BOOKS

FRANK ASCH — *BEAR SHADOW*
RUTH BROWN — *A DARK DARK TALE*
TARO GOMI — *SHADOWS*
LIZ AND DICK WILMES — *GREGORY GROUNDHOG*
(Found in MAKE-TAKE GAMES.)

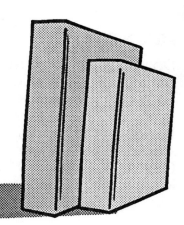

S
C
I
E
N
C
E

IN THE SKY

ATTACH BLUE BUTCHER PAPER TO THE CEILING OVER THE CIRCLE TIME AREA. HAVE THE CHILDREN LIE ON THE FLOOR LOOKING UP. SAY SOMETHING LIKE, *"PRETEND IT IS A BEAUTIFUL DAY AND YOU ARE RESTING OUTSIDE LOOKING AT ALL OF THE THINGS IN THE SKY."* LET THE CHILDREN THINK AND THEN SAY, *"WHAT DID YOU SEE?"* ENCOURAGE THE CHILDREN TO TALK ABOUT ALL OF THE THINGS THEY SAW, BOTH NATURAL AND MAN-MADE.

SEVERAL DAYS LATER TAKE THE DAYTIME SKY DOWN AND HANG BLACK PAPER FOR THE NIGHT SKY. REPEAT THE ACTIVITY.
EXTENSION:
ADD THE NATURAL AND MAN-MADE THINGS THEY SEE TO THE DAY/NIGHT SKY.

FINGERPLAYS

RING AROUND THE ROCKET SHIP
(tune: Ring Around the Rosie)

Ring around the rocket ship.
Try to grab a star.
Stardust, stardust
Fall where you are.

MOON RIDE

Do you want to go up with me to the moon?
Let's get in our rocket ship and blast off soon!
Faster and faster we reach to the sky.
Isn't it fun to be able to fly?
We're on the moon, now all take a look.
And gently sit down and we'll read a book.
(Read GOOD NIGHT MOON by Margaret Wise Brown)

FINGERPLAYS

BEND AND STRETCH

Bend and stretch, reach for the stars.
There goes Jupiter, here comes Mars.

Bend and stretch, reach for the sky.
Stand on tip-e-toe, oh! so high!

BOOM, BANG!

Boom, bang, boom, bang!
Rumpety, lumpety, bump!
Zoom, zam, zoom, zam!
Clippety, clappety, clump.

Rustles and bustles
And swishes and zings!
What a wonderful sight
A lightening bolt brings!

HOLD ON TIGHT

Hold on tight, we're flying through
  the stars,
There goes Jupiter, here comes Mars.
Fly so high, floating in the sky.
Our magic carpet is flying high.
(Read this as the children pretend
they are on a magic carpet.)

TWINKLE, TWINKLE LITTLE STAR

Twinkle, twinkle, little star,
How I wonder where you are.
Up above the world so high,
Like a diamond in the sky.
Twinkle, twinkle, little star.
How I wonder where you are.

SNACK

ASTRONAUT SHAKES
YOU'LL NEED
3 8oz cartons of plain yogurt
3 very ripe bananas
1 1/2 cups of cold apple juice
1 1/2 cups of cold milk
3T honey (optional)

TO MAKE: Combine the yogurt and bananas in a blender and mix them until they are smooth. Pour the mixture into a large pitcher and stir in the juice and milk. Add a little honey to taste. As you are drinking your shakes take an imaginary trip through space.

FIELD TRIPS

- Each day on your way to school look at the clouds. See how they look and how they are moving - fast, slowly, not at all. During the day take the children outside   and have them look at the clouds. Talk about them. Do this several times so that the children see different types of cloud formations.

147

SCIENCE

LANGUAGE GAMES

I WISH Have the children close their eyes, pretend it is night and say the *I WISH* rhyme. When you've finished have several children make wishes. Repeat the rhyme and let several more children make wishes. Continue.
EXTENSION:
Write each child's wish on individual construction paper stars or on one giant posterboard star.

> ### I WISH
> *I wish I may, I wish I might
> Have the wish I wish tonight.*

TRIP TO THE MOON Cut out a giant moon shape from yellow posterboard. Bring it, a marker, and a suitcase to circle time. Say to the children, *"Let's pretend that we are astronauts and take a trip to the moon. (Open up the suitcase.) We can only bring one suitcase for all of us, so each person can only take one thing."* Have each person tell what he would take along and come up and pretend to put it in the suitcase. As each child is putting his `thing' in the suitcase write what he says on the moon. When you're finished, hang the moon from the ceiling.
EXTENSION:
Share the list with parents in your next newsletter.

SUN FUN Using yellow posterboard make a large sun with lots of rays. Ask the children what they like to do on hot sunny days. Write their ideas on the rays of the sun. Remember you can easily use both sides. Hang it next to the moon. (See *TRIP TO THE MOON*.)

CLOUD SEARCH On a day when the sky is full of big billowy clouds, go outside and play *CLOUD SEARCH*. Give each child a pair of toilet paper binoculars, have them lie or sit on the ground, and search the clouds for animals. As children find animals, have them tell what and where the animals are. On other days, have the children search for another category of things such as foods, flowers, faces, etc.

ACTIVE GAMES

IF YOU WERE A CLOUD

Pretend that the classroom is the sky. Have each child think about how he would move if he were a cloud. Ask the children, *"Who wants to be a slow moving cloud that is just floating along? Those who do start floating."*

Have the other children be the wind taking deep breaths and slowly and quietly blowing the clouds around. After a while, change clouds. Ask, *"Who wants to be a rain cloud racing through the sky to dump water on the fields? Those who do get ready."* Have the others be the strong winds pushing them along. Continue in this manner with stagnant clouds and almost no wind, big billowy clouds on a windy day, etc.

RUN FOR THE SUN

Get a yellow beach ball and pretend that it is the sun. Play this game inside or out. Have the children stand in a group. In an open area roll the sun across the floor. Call on 2 children and the group says, *"Run for the sun."* The 2 children run after the sun, pick it up together, bring it back to the group, and give it to a child in the group. That child rolls the sun and you name 2 more children as the group says, *"Run for the sun."* Continue having fun chasing the sun over and over again as it rolls through the sky.

BOOKS

MARGARET WISE BROWN — *GOODNIGHT MOON*
GAIL GIBBONS — *SUN UP, SUN DOWN*
CHARLES SHAW — *IT LOOKED LIKE SPILT MILK*
TOMIE DePAOLA — *CLOUD BOOK*
JANE YOLEN — *OWL MOON*
HARRIET ZIEFERT — *SARAH'S DREAM*

SCIENCE

BUBBLES

FOR OPENERS

TEACH THE CHILDREN THE BUBBLE SONG AND THEN EVERYONE SING IT WHILE DOING THE ACTIONS. REPEAT SEVERAL TIMES SO THAT ALL OF THE CHILDREN CAN MOVE LIKE BUBBLES TWO OR THREE TIMES.

THE BUBBLE SONG

1 little, 2 little, 3 little bubbles (Tap 9 children on heads.)
4 little, 5 little, 6 little bubbles
7 little, 8 little, 9 little bubbles
Floating all around.

9 little, 8 little, 7 little bubbles (Tap again.)
6 little, 5 little, 4 little bubbles
3 little, 2 little, 1 little bubble
Bursting on the ground.

LIZ WILMES

FINGERPLAYS

HERE'S A BUBBLE
(Adapted from traditional rhyme.)

Here's a bubble,
And here's a bubble,
A great big bubble I see.

Shall we count them?
Are you ready?
1, 2, 3!

BLOW YOUR BUBBLES
(tune: Row, Row, Row Your Boat)

Blow, blow, blow your bubbles,
Blow them all around.
Blow them up and blow them down,
Blow them all around.
Liz Wilmes

150

SNACK

MELON BALL BUBBLES
YOU'LL NEED
Several different melons

TO MAKE: Clean each melon. Using a melon scoop, let the children make melon balls and put them in a large dish. Carefully stir them.

FIELD TRIP

● On a sunny day take a bottle of bubble solution and several wands with you on a walk around your neighborhood. As soon as you get outside blow some bubbles. Watch them float away. Where are they going? Keep walking. Blow some more. Look for a big one. Did it pop? Keep walking. Blow again. What colors can you see in the bubbles? Keep walking. If you get to an open area, blow again and see if you can catch any of the bubbles. Did you? What happened?

BUBBLE SOLUTION RECIPES

BUBBLE BREW I
YOU'LL NEED
2 quarts water
1 cup liquid detergent
  (Joy or Dawn)
1 T sugar
2 T glycerine

TO MAKE: Mix with the children in a large bowl and let stand for at least three hours. Store in the refrigerator.

BUBBLE BREW II
YOU'LL NEED
1 quart water
3/4 cup liquid detergent
  (Joy or Dawn)
1/4 cup corn syrup

TO MAKE: Mix with the children in a large bowl and let stand for at least 6 hours. Store in refrigerator.

SCIENCE

LANGUAGE GAMES

BLOWING BUBBLES

Bring to circle time, a large low pan like an aluminum baking dish, a pitcher of water, liquid detergent, and a straw for each child. Set the pan on the floor in the middle of the group. Slowly pour the water into the pan. Give several children straws and have them blow into the water. What happened? Did the bubbles last a long time?

Add a little detergent to the water. Give several more children straws and have them very slowly blow the water. Any bubbles? Large or small? Add a little more detergent and let several more children blow. Now what is happening?

EXTENSIONS:

● Put the pan on a table and let the children keep blowing during free choice. How high can they get the bubbles to rise?

● **Make Bubble Bottles**: Fill 16oz plastic soda bottles about half full of water. Add a little food coloring and liquid dish detergent to each one. (Joy and Dawn work well.) Set them on a tray for the children to shake and create bubbles.

NAME A COLOR

Bring a bottle of commercial bubble solution and a wand to circle time. Blow a bubble/s. As the bubble/s floats, point to different children and have them each call out a color in the bubble. Let a child blow the next bubble. Once again take turns and call out colors in the bubble/s. Continue, letting several more children blow bubbles.

BUBBLE BUCKET

Using different colors of colored construction paper, cut out tiny, small, big, and giant size bubbles. Back each one with felt or magnetic tape. Put the bubbles in a bucket. Bring it and the felt/magnet board to circle time.

Have a child reach into the bucket, pull out a bubble, and put it on the board. Have the others call out, "*tiny, small, big, or giant.*" Ask what color bubble it is. Continue, letting other children pull bubbles out of the bucket.

ACTIVE GAMES

BUBBLE TRIPS   Have each child close his eyes and pretend that he is a bubble floating to a special place. Open their eyes. Say, *"All of you bubbles, time to take off and float away."* (Slowly walk around the group and blow on the children.) As you blow they should get up and begin to floating like bubbles. After a while say, *"Time to float back home."* (Bubbles float back.) Have each `bubble' tell you what special place he floated to.

        On other days let the `bubbles' take special trips. For example, they could float to the zoo to see their favorite animals, to the store to buy their favorite foods, to a garden to rest on different colored flowers, and so on.

LAZY BUBBLES   Have the children pretend that they are different types of bubbles moving through the air.
- Lazy bubbles slowly moving from tree to tree.
- Busy bubbles bouncing along the sidewalk.
- Scared bubbles dodging the `bubble monster'.
- Happy bubbles rolling to a party.
- Continue.

CATCH BUBBLES   Name 3-4 children. Have them stand up. Blow bubbles into the air. Let those children try to catch bubbles on their hands or arms. Everyone clap for them. Name several more children, blow some bubbles, and let the children catch them. Repeat over and over.

BOOKS

MERCER MAYER — *BUBBLE BUBBLE*

153

SCIENCE

ROCKS/STONES

GO ON A STONE SEARCH WALK AROUND THE NEIGHBORHOOD. BRING A TOTE BAG. AS YOU WALK EVERYONE LOOK FOR ALL TYPES OF STONES. WHENEVER A CHILD FINDS ONE, HAVE HIM PICK IT UP AND PUT IT IN THE TOTE.

WHEN YOU GET BACK TO THE CENTER, DUMP THE STONES OUT ON A PIECE OF POSTERBOARD. TALK ABOUT THE COLLECTION.

- FIND THE LARGEST/SMALLEST
- ROUND ONES/POINTED ONES
- SMOOTH/BUMPY
- CLEAN/DIRTY

EXTENSION: PUT WATER IN YOUR SAND/WATER TABLE. ADD THE STONE COLLECTION TO IT.

SNACK

PEBBLES
YOU'LL NEED
Raisins
Peanuts
Different round cereals such as Kix

TO MAKE: Let the children pour the different ingredients in a bowl and then mix them up with a spoon. Pass the bowl and have the children use a small clean shovel to scoop some `pebbles' on their plates. Enjoy with apple wedges.

FINGERPLAYS

BULLFROG
Here's Mr. Bullfrog
Sitting on a rock.
Along comes a little boy.
Mr. Bullfrog jumps, KERPLOP!

LANGUAGE GAMES

1	2	3
4	5	6
7	8	9

STONE TOSS

On an old white sheet draw a giant 9' square with permanent marker. Write a numeral in each square. Have several stones. Have the children sit around the sheet. Give the stones to different children. Everyone call out, *"Toss."* The children toss their stones onto the sheet. Pick up each stone and let everyone name the numeral it had landed on. Give the stones to different children and play *`STONE TOSS'* again and again.

LOAD THE TRUCK

Bring a dump truck, a small bucket of pebbles and a little scoop to circle time. Give a child the scoop and have him dip it into the bucket to get as many pebbles as he can. Take the pebbles off of the scoop one at a time and count them as you load the truck. Continue to scoop and have everyone count until the truck is loaded.

LISTEN CAREFULLY

Get a stone along with a piece of wood (block), a bowl of water, a piece of metal (cookie sheet), a sponge, and a sheet of hard plastic. Lay all of the objects except the stone on the floor. Drop the stone on each one. Have the children listen and call out what the stone landed on.

Now have the children cover their eyes with a hand. Tell them to listen carefully. Drop the stone on one of the objects. Uncover their eyes and name the object. Drop the stone on the object again. Were the sounds the same?

155

LANGUAGE GAMES

FEEL IT

Get a variety of rocks, pebbles, and stones. Put them in a bag. Pass the bag to a child, have him pull one out and keep it in his hand without looking at it. Feel it and tell the others one thing about it—size, texture, characteristic, etc. Open his hand, show his rock to the others, and set it on a tray. Continue until all of the rocks are on the tray.

EXTENSION:

Set the tray of rocks and a magnifying glass on a special table for further examination.

PET ROCKS

Have children bring a favorite rock, stone, or pebble to school. Put each one on a piece of posterboard with the child's name. Using the sample diagram, make a 'Pet Rock Chart.' Over the next several days during free choice, write what each child says about his rock on the chart.

After the children have told about their rocks, bring the chart and rocks to circle time. Hold up each rock and have the child tell the others where he found it. Using the information on the chart you tell several other facts about each one.

Names	Found	Feel	Size	Color	Shape
John's Rock	Lawn	Bumpy	Small	yellow/brown	Long Pointed
Betty's Rock	Sidewalk	Sharp	Medium	White	Pointed
Matt's Rock	Dirt pile	Smooth	Small	White	Round
Seth's Rock	Parking lot	Smooth	Big	red brown	Round

WHAT'S NEXT?

Get 8-10 small, medium, and large stones. Put them in 3 separate piles for the children to see. Using a particular pattern, such as small-medium-large, small-medium-large, small-medium-? begin to make a row of stones. As you're making the row, say the pattern aloud. After making several repetitions, stop. Ask the children what size stone comes next. Complete the row. Put the stones back and play WHAT'S NEXT again with a new series of stones.

ACTIVE GAMES

ROCK 'N ROLL   Have the children sit on the floor as if they were rocks. When you say, *"Roll"* the children should tumble around the floor. When you say, *"Rock"* they should sit upright again like a rock. Continue *ROCK 'N ROLLING* using as much floor space as is safe.

BOOKS

MARCIA BROWN — *STONE SOUP*
WILLIAM STEIG — *SYLVESTOR AND THE MAGIC PEBBLE*

DAY & NIGHT

FOR OPENERS

PLAY `DAY AND NIGHT' WITH THE CHILDREN. TO PLAY SAY SOMETHING ABOUT DAY OR NIGHT SUCH AS, *"I WEAR PAJAMAS AT _____."* LET THE CHILDREN COMPLETE THE SENTENCE BY CLOSING THEIR EYES IF IT IS NIGHT, OPENING THEIR EYES IF IT IS DAY, AND BLINKING QUICKLY IF IT IS BOTH. CONTINUE WITH DIFFERENT DAY AND NIGHT ACTIVITIES.

- I SLEEP FOR A LONG TIME DURING THE _____.
- I EAT BREAKFAST DURING THE _____.
- IT IS DARK DURING THE _____.
- THE STARS SHINE DURING THE _____.
- I PLAY DURING THE _____.
- I GET DRESSED DURING THE _____.
- I BRUSH MY TEETH DURING THE _____.
- CONTINUE

FINGERPLAYS

GOOD MORNING

Good morning merry sunshine.
How are you today?
I've come to my school
To laugh and sing and play.

GOOD NIGHT

Before I jump into my bed,
Before I dim the light,
I put my shoes together,
So they can talk at night.

I'm sure they would be lonesome,
If I tossed one here and there,
So I put them close together,
For they're a friendly pair.

SHHHHH!

Shhhhh —- be very quiet.
Shhhhh —- be very still.

Cross you busy, busy arms,
Close your sleepy, sleepy eyes,

Shhhhh —- be very still.
Good night!

NAPTIME

I'm sleepy, very sleepy.
I want to yawn and stretch.
I'll close my eyes and just pretend
That daylight time has gone.

SNACK

MOON SANDWICHES
YOU'LL NEED
Apples
Peanut butter
Raisins

TO MAKE: Wash the apples and cut them into moon shaped wedges. Spread each `moon` with peanut butter and then add the raisin `craters` to each one.

LANGUAGE GAMES

NIGHT TIME ACTIVITIES

Have the children close their eyes, pretend that it is night time, and think of things they like to do while it is dark outside. Open their eyes and talk about their ideas. On another day talk about things the children like to do while it is light outside.

EXTENSION:

Write their night time activities on a giant `Star Wheel`. To make your wheel, cut a giant posterboard circle and star approximately the same diameter. Cut a 2"x4" rectangle opening in one of the points of the star. Write the children's ideas around the edge of the circle. Attach the circle behind the star with a metal brad. Slowly turn the wheel and read everyone's ideas as they `shine` in the opening. Repeat the idea using a sun for daytime ideas.

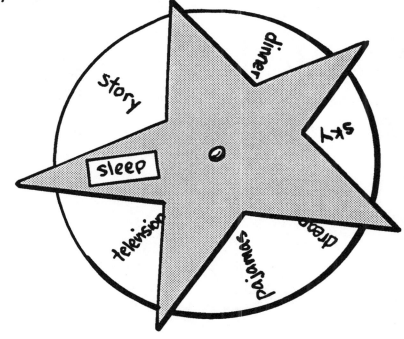

SCIENCE

159

LANGUAGE GAMES

PICTURE SORT   Cut a 12"x12" piece of yellow (daytime) and black (night time) posterboard. Find magazine pictures of activities going on during the day and the night. Set the boards on the floor. Hold up a picture. Talk about what is going on and then decide if it is a day or night activity. Give the picture to a child and have him set it on the daytime or night time board. Continue with the remaining pictures.

GOOD MORNING   Have the children yawn and stretch as if they were just waking up. Talk about all of the things that the children do when they first get out of bed. Include all of the ways the children might say "*Good Morning*" to each of their family members.
Play *GOOD NIGHT* in a similar manner, including all of the activities children do just before going to bed.

PAJAMA DAY   A week or so before *PAJAMA DAY* write a note to the families asking them to have their children wear pajamas over their clothes on the specific day.

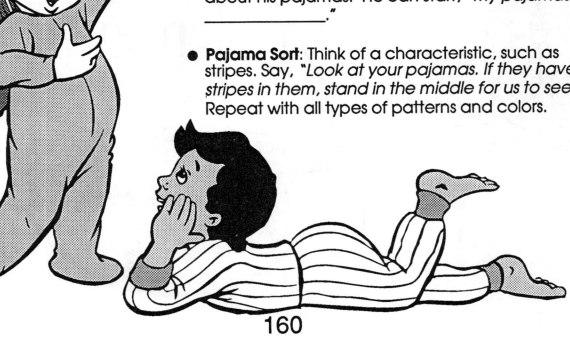

- **Pajama Fashion Show**: Describe a pair of pajamas. When a child recognizes his pajamas, he should stand up and parade around. Everyone clap. Continue with all the pajamas.

- **My Pajamas**: Have each child tell one thing about his pajamas. He can start, "*My pajamas _____.*"

- **Pajama Sort**: Think of a characteristic, such as stripes. Say, "*Look at your pajamas. If they have stripes in them, stand in the middle for us to see.*" Repeat with all types of patterns and colors.

160

ACTIVE GAMES

PET PANTOMIME   Have the children sit in a circle with lots of space in the middle. Each child thinks of a stuffed animal he takes or would like to take to bed. Call on a child. He moves, wiggles, and talks like his stuffed animal. The others guess what animal he takes to bed.

SCIENCE

BOOKS

CYNTHIA RYLANT — *NIGHT IN THE COUNTRY*
NORMA SIMON — *WHERE DOES MY CAT SLEEP?*
MARGARET WISE BROWN — *GOOD NIGHT MOON*

DANDELIONS

PLAY `I SEE YELLOW` WITH THE CHILDREN. BRING A REAL DANDELION OR MAKE ONE BY CRUSHING UP A PIECE OF YELLOW TISSUE PAPER AND GLUING IT TO A POPSICLE STICK.

TELL THE CHILDREN TO LOOK AROUND THE ROOM FOR YELLOW OBJECTS. GIVE THE DANDELION TO A CHILD. HAVE HIM HOLD IT AND SAY, "I SEE A YELLOW (BOOK) ON THE BOOKSHELF." TELL THE CHILD TO HAND THE DANDELION TO SOMEONE ELSE. THAT CHILD TAKES THE DANDELION AND NAMES ANOTHER YELLOW OBJECT. NOW SAY TO THE GROUP, "WE HAVE NAMED TWO YELLOW OBJECTS, A BOOK AND A_____." (LET THE GROUP COMPLETE THE SENTENCE) GIVE THE DANDELION TO A THIRD CHILD AND CONTINUE THE GAME.

FINGERPLAYS

DANDELION SEEDS

In a dandelion flower
Very snug and warm,
Baby seeds are hiding
Safe from harm.

Pick the fuzzy dandelion.
Hold it way up high.
Come, Mr. Wind
Help the seeds to fly.

DROOPING DANDELIONS

Five little dandelions
Standing in the sun.
See their heads nodding
Bowing one by one.

Down, down, down
Falls the gentle rain,
And the five little dandelions
Lift up their heads again!

DANDELION PLAY

If I were a dandelion
Sleeping underneath the ground,
I'd raise my head and grow and grow,
And stretch by arms and grow and grow,
And nod my head and say,
"I'm glad to see you all today." (Nod to each
    other.)

DANDELION CRADLES

In their little cradles, packed in tight,
Dandelion seeds are sleeping out of sight.
Mr. Wind comes blowing with all his might.
The dandelion seeds are scattered left and
    right.

162

SNACK

DANDELION CRACKERS
YOU'LL NEED
Round crackers
Yellow cheese slices
Green pepper slices

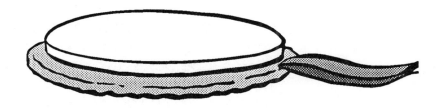

TO MAKE: Using cookie cutters, cut the cheese slices into dandelion circles. Put one `dandelion' on each cracker. Serve them with green pepper stems.

FIELD TRIP

- Walk to a public field or park and let the children pick bouquets of dandelions. Put them in styrofoam cups. Carry the bouquets back to the center, add water to each bouquet, and set them around the room. Put a magnifying glass near several of the dandelion bouquets so children can examine them more closely.

LANGUAGE GAMES

EXPLORE A DANDELION

Give each child a dandelion. Using your senses learn all you can about dandelions. Discuss your ideas.

- *"Look at your dandelion. What do you see?"*
- *"Smell your dandelion. What does it smell like?"*
- *"Rub the dandelion on the palm of your hand. How does it feel?"*
- *"Hold the dandelion near your ear. What is it saying?"*
- *"Do you eat dandelions? Not really. They need to be fixed in a special way."*

SCIENCE

163

LANGUAGE GAMES

WHICH DANDELION ?

Cut between 5-10 large yellow construction paper dandelions. Number each one beginning with 1. String a rope across two chairs. Using clothespins clip the dandelions to the rope. Point to each one and have the children count them together.

Give a child directions telling him to pick a certain dandelion and give it to someone else. For example, *"Jo Ellen pick dandelion number 4 and give it to Sequita."* *"Moranda, pick the fifth dandelion and give it to Barbara."* Continue until all of the dandelions have been picked. Give the directions in reverse and have the children clip the dandelions back on the rope. For example, *"Sequita, give your number 4 dandelion to Sam. Sam, clip it back on the rope."*

After all of the dandelions are clipped back on the rope, put them in order.

LISTEN CAREFULLY

Say *"dandelion"* over and over, every once in a while saying the name of a different flower. As soon as the children hear the flower, they should call it out. For example, *"Dandelion, dandelion, dandelion, dandelion, tulip, dandelion, rose,"* etc.

DANDELIONS EVERYWHERE

field garden
park
grass
dirt
sidewalk
driveway

Tell the children to think of all of the places that they have seen dandelions. Say this rhyme over and over and have them fill in the blank with a different place each time.

DANDELIONS EVERYWHERE

Dandelions, dandelions growing everywhere
I found one in the _____. (Children name a place)

And picked it with care.

EXTENSION:
Cut a giant yellow posterboard dandelion. Bring it and a marker to circle time and write all of the places the children found dandelions on it. Hang it at the children's eye level.

ACTIVE GAMES

PASS THE DANDELION

Bring a real dandelion or one you've made to circle time. (See *FOR OPENERS*) Teach your children the *DANDELION SONG* and then add the actions. Once they understand the game, sing the song faster and faster.

> *DANDELION SONG*
> (tune: Mary Had a Little Lamb)
> (Child's name) *has a dandelion, dandelion, dandelion* (Give a dandelion to the child.)
> (Child's name) *has a dandelion*
> *And passes it to* (Child's name). (Child gives dandelion to another child and all say the name.)

SCIENCE

BOOKS

LORNA BALIAN — *AMINAL*
BARRIE WATTS — *DANDELION*

MAGNETS

PLAY *"YES-NO"* WITH THE CHILDREN. HAVE A MAGNET AND A BASKET OF OBJECTS, SOME OF WHICH ARE MAGNETIC AND SOME OF WHICH ARE NOT. DIVIDE A PIECE OF POSTERBOARD IN HALF. WRITE *"YES"* AT THE TOP OF ONE SIDE AND *"NO"* AT THE TOP OF THE OTHER.

 HAVE A CHILD COME UP, PULL AN OBJECT OUT OF THE BASKET, AND ATTACH IT TO THE MAGNET. IF IT STICKS, HAVE EVERYONE CALL OUT `YES' AND SET IT ON THE `YES' SIDE OF THE BOARD; IF NOT, SAY `NO' AND SET IT ON THE `NO' SIDE OF THE BOARD. CONTINUE UNTIL ALL OF THE OBJECTS HAVE BEEN SORTED.

FIELD TRIPS

● Take a basket of magnets with you when you go outside. While the children are playing, have them use the different magnets to `test' the outside equipment and environment. Before going back inside gather the children and name all of the things which were and were not magnetic.

166

SNACK

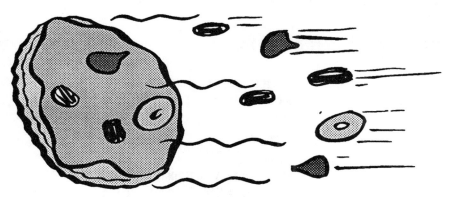

MAGNETIC CRACKERS
YOU'LL NEED
Crackers
Peanut butter
Spreadable cheese
Variety of cereals
Raisins
Carob chips

TO MAKE: Let children `magnetize' their crackers by spreading them with peanut butter and cheese. Set the `magnet crackers' on a plate. Put the different toppings in individual bowls. When you serve snack, let the children choose which toppings they want to `attract' to their magnetic crackers.

LANGUAGE GAMES

COUNT THE CLIPS
Put some large metal paper clips and some plastic paper clips in a margarine tub. Mix them up. Hold a magnet in the tub and pull it up. Show it to the children. Did you catch any of the paper clips? Pull them off one at a time, counting as you go. Let a child come up to the tub, catch some clips, and then everyone count how many he caught. Continue with other children catching clips and everyone counting them.
EXTENSION:
Make a chart of how many clips each child caught.

PREDICT AND CHECK
Before circle time have the children search the classroom for small objects which they think will and will not magnetize. Put all of the objects in a special box.
Bring a magnet and the box to circle time. Pull the objects out one at a time. Hold each one up and have the children predict if it will magnetize. Then check their prediction by holding it to the magnet. After checking each one, have a child put the object back where it belongs.

167

ACTIVE GAMES

BODY MAGNETS Pair off the children. Have one child in each pair hold his hand out to be the magnet. The other child is the magnetic object. When you say, "*Magnetize your elbow,*" he sticks his elbow to the magnet. Continue naming different parts. Switch roles and play `BODY MAGNETS' again.

VARIATION:

Instead of naming a body part to magnetize, just say, "*Magnetize.*" Each child should magnetize any body part he chooses. Go around the group and let each magnet name the body part which is sticking to him. Say, "*Let go*" and the magnetic object drops off of his magnet. Repeat several times encouraging the children to attach different parts of their bodies. Switch roles and play some more.

BOOKS

FRANK BRANLEY — *MICKEY'S MAGNET*

168

DINOSAURS

FOR OPENERS

USING THE DINOSAUR PATTERNS MAKE POSTERBOARD STICK PUPPETS. BRING THEM TO CIRCLE TIME. HOLD UP THE PUPPETS AND INTRODUCE EACH DINOSAUR TO THE CHILDREN. TELL THE CHILDREN THAT THEY CAN TAKE `DINOSAUR RIDES' ON THEIR FAVORITE DINOSAURS. THEN ASK, *"WHO WOULD LIKE TO RIDE THE TYRANNOSAURS?"* (GIVE THAT PUPPET TO ONE OF THE CHILDREN.) ASK ABOUT EACH OF THE OTHERS AND HAND THE DINOSAURS OUT. AS THE CHILDREN RIDE THEIR DINOSAURS THE OTHERS VERY SLOWLY SING *"WE'RE RIDING OUR DINOSAURS."*

WE'RE RIDING OUR DINOSAURS
(TUNE: FARMER IN THE DELL)

WE'RE RIDING OUT DINOSAURS,
WE'RE RIDING OUR DINOSAURS
UP AND DOWN, SIDE TO SIDE.
WE'RE RIDING OUR DINOSAURS.

WE'RE RESTING OUR DINOSAURS,
WE'RE RESTING OUR DINOSAURS
SIT BACK DOWN, CROSS YOUR LEGS
WE'RE RESTING OUR DINOSAURS.
  LIZ WILMES

AFTER THE SONG EACH CHILD TELLS THE OTHERS WHERE HE AND HIS DINOSAUR WENT. REPEAT A NUMBER OF TIMES SO THAT ALL OF THE CHILDREN CAN TAKE SEVERAL RIDES.

SCIENCE

Pteranodon

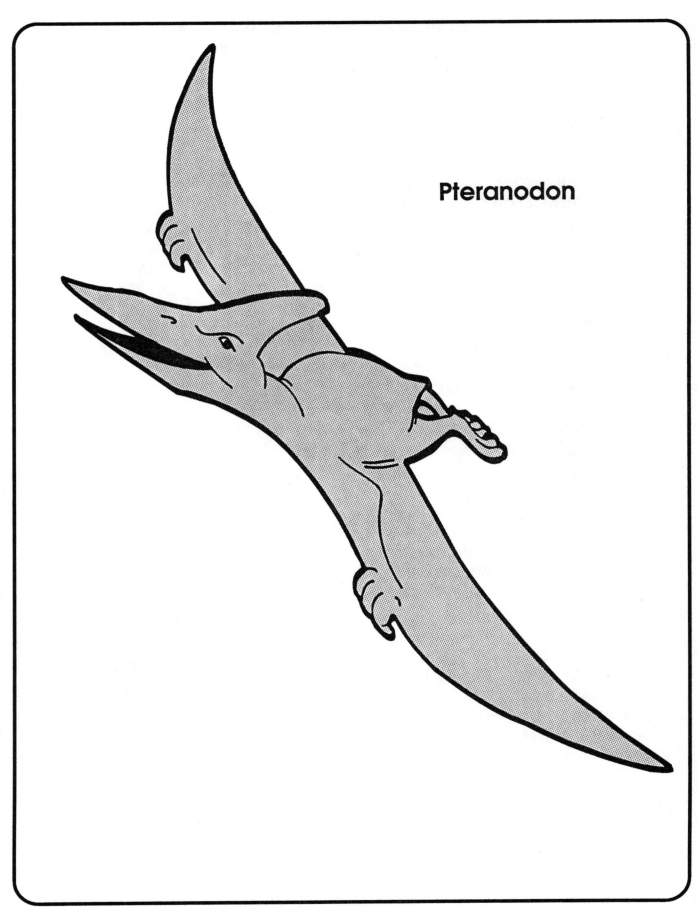

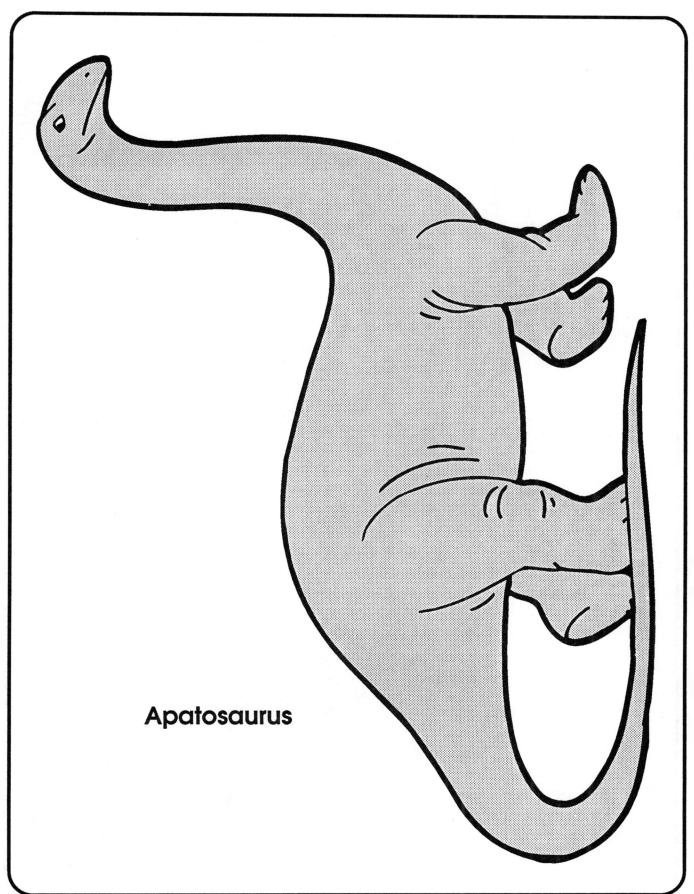

Apatosaurus

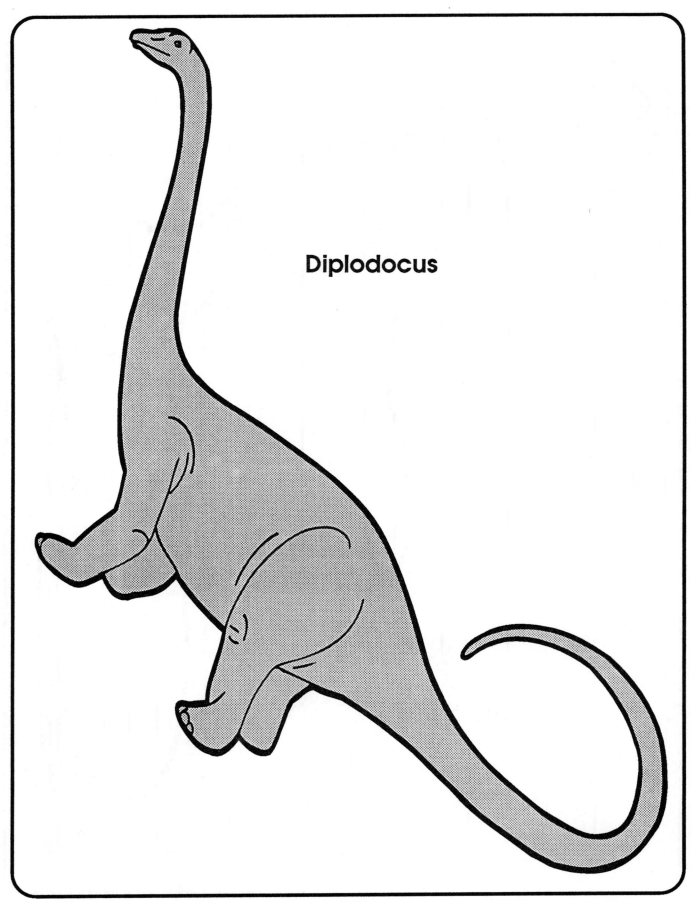

Diplodocus

Tyrannosaurus

Triceratops

Stegosaurus

SNACK

DINOSAUR SNACKS

YOU'LL NEED:
Carrots
Celery
Broccoli
Cauliflower

TO MAKE: Clean and carefully cut the vegetables into small pieces. Put them on a plate. Have the children pretend that they are one of the vegetarian dinosaurs as they eat snack. (Stegosaurus, Apatosaurus, Triceratops, Diplodocus)

LANGUAGE GAMES

WHICH ONE DOESN'T BELONG

Make 4-5 of each type of dinosaur out of the same color construction paper or posterboard. Back each one with felt or a piece of magnet tape.

Bring the dinosaurs and your felt/magnet board to circle time. Put one of each type of dinosaur on the board. Identify and talk about each one with the children. Clear the board.

Have the children cover their eyes. Put a series of 4-5 dinosaurs on the board, all but one of which are identical. Have the children open their eyes, look at the dinosaurs, and pick the one which is not like the others. Take it off of the board. Have the children close their eyes again, put up a new series, and continue as above.

VARIATIONS:

- Put 4-5 dinosaurs on the board, only two of which are the same. Have the children choose the twins.
- Put 4-5 felt dinosaurs on the board, all of which are identical. Have several different felt features, such as a toenail, mouth, and eye. Have the children cover their eyes. Add a feature to one of the dinosaurs. Open their eyes. Which dinosaur has the feature? (First, second, third, fourth, or fifth one? What feature is it?)

DINOSAUR ECHO

Name a dinosaur and have the children say it back. Repeat with other dinosaur names. Another time have the children echo back using a whisper, gruff, squeaky, or loud voice.

LANGUAGE GAMES

WHERE ARE THE DINOSAURS?

Make 3 dinosaur headbands. Put 3 chairs in the circle time area. Pretend that one is a mountain, one is a tree, and one is a lake.

Give 3 children headbands to wear. Give each one directions where to move, such as *"Triceratops Pat walk to the mountain."* (He does.) When he gets there he can position himself anyplace near the mountain he wants. He freezes there. After all of the dinosaurs are in place, the other children tell exactly where each one is in relation to the object, such as, *"Triceratops Pat is <u>on top</u> of the mountain. Stegosaurus Sally is <u>behind</u> the tree. Tyrannosaurs Nicole is <u>under</u> the water."* After talking about each one, say, *"Time to go home dinosaurs."* Repeat with other children.

TALK ABOUT

Hold up a picture or model of each type of dinosaur. Talk about the different characteristics of each one.

- **Apatosaurus** used to be called Brontosaurus. It was a vegetarian who fed mainly from the treetops because of its very long neck.

- **Diplodocus** was one of the longest dinosaurs, having a very long neck and tail, but a short body. It was a vegetarian who ate from tree tops.

- **Pterananodon** was a large flying reptile. It lived in cliffs near water and fed mainly on fish. It had a very wide wing span, much like a glider.

- **Stegosaurus** was a vegetarian. Its head was very low to the ground and thus it ate mostly ground cover. It had large bony plates along its back and four spikes on the end of his tail to use for defense.

- **Tyrannosaurus** was an enormous dinosaur, with a huge jaw and long sharp teeth. It had strong hind legs and very short forearms for balance. It was a meat eater.

- **Triceratops** had a huge head with three horns protruding from the face — one was a nose and the other two were horns on its forehead. Triceratops was a plant eater.

ACTIVE GAMES

DINOSAUR HUNT Before circle time hide posterboard or rubber dinosaurs all over the room. Talk with the children about the fact that dinosaurs are now extinct. Special scientists called paleontologists, study dinosaurs. They find dinosaur skeletons buried deep in the ground. Carefully these scientists dig the dinosaurs out and study their bones.

Let the children be paleontologists and search for dinosaurs. When all have been found name each type.

EXTENSION:

Bury rubber dinosaurs in the sand table or in the sand area outside.

BOOKS

ALIKI — *MY VISIT TO THE DINOSAURS*
CAROL CARRICK — *PATRICK'S DINOSAURS*
SYD HOFF — *DANNY AND THE DINOSAUR*

COMMUNITY WORKERS

FOR OPENERS

TELL THE CHILDREN A RIDDLE ABOUT A COMMUNITY
WORKER. HAVE THEM CALL OUT WHO THEY THINK IT IS.
ASK THE CHILDREN IF THEY KNOW ANYONE WHO
REALLY DOES THAT JOB. WHO? WHERE DOES
THE PERSON WORK? HERE ARE A FEW STARTERS.

I LIKE BOOKS.
I HELP PEOPLE FIND THE BOOKS THAT THEY WANT.
I CHECK OUT THEIR BOOKS AT MY DESK.
WHO AM I?

I USE A HAMMER AND A SAW.
I BUILD LARGE AND SMALL HOUSES.
WHO AM I?

I TAKE YOUR FOOD ORDER WHEN YOU COME INTO MY
      RESTAURANT.
I BRING YOUR FOOD AFTER IT IS COOKED.
SOMETIMES YOU LEAVE ME A TIP.
WHO AM I?

I WATCH PEOPLE SWIM.
SOMETIMES I WALK AROUND THE SWIMMING POOL.
IF SOMEONE IS STRUGGLING IN THE WATER, I DIVE IN AND
      SWIM AS FAST AS I CAN TO HELP HIM.
WHO AM I?

OCCUPATIONS

FINGERPLAYS

THE COBBLER

*Crooked heels and scruffy toes
Are all the kinds of shoes he knows.
He patches up the broken places,
Sews the seams and shines their faces.*

A HOUSE FOR ME

*The carpenter's hammer goes rap, rap, rap.
The carpenter's saw goes saw-see, saw-see.
He hammers and hammers and saws and saws,
Building a house for you and me.*

FARMER PLOWS THE GROUND
(tune: Here We Go 'Round the Mulberry Bush)

*First the farmer plows the ground,
Plows the ground, plows the ground.
First the farmer plows the ground,
Then he plants the seeds.*

Next the farmer plants the seeds,
....
So that they will grow.

The rain and sun will help them grow,
....
Right up through the ground.

Last the farmer picks the beans,
....
And we have food to eat.

SCHOOL WORKERS

*This little worker drives us to school everyday.
This little worker helps us work and play.*

*This little worker mops our school floor.
This little worker brings mail to our door.*

*This little worker keeps our papers in a file.
Thank you every worker for doing your job with a smile*
  Liz Wilmes

SNACKS

STOP SIGNS
YOU'LL NEED
Eight-sided crackers
Peanut butter
Natural red jam

TO MAKE: Spread a thin
layer of peanut butter
on each cracker and
then top it with red
jam.

YIELD SIGNS
YOU'LL NEED
Triangle crackers
Yellow cheese

TO MAKE: Cut the
yellow cheese into
triangles. Put the
cheese on the
crackers.

STOP AND GO LIGHTS
YOU'LL NEED
Rectangular crackers
Strawberries
Yellow cheese
Green olives

TO MAKE: Slice the
strawberries, cheese,
and olives into circles.
Let the children put
them on the crackers in
the right order.

CLASSROOM VISITOR

- In your next parent newsletter invite your parents to visit the class and tell the children about their work. Ask them to wear their work clothes, bring any tools they use, and/or show pictures of their work or products.

FIELD TRIP

- Take a walk around your neighborhood. As you walk look for adults who are working. Stop and watch them. What are they doing? How are they helping the community? Do you know any of the workers?

181

OCCUPATIONS

LANGUAGE GAMES

WHEN I GO TO WORK

Get a clear plastic photo cube. Slip pictures of different workers into the sides. Roll the cube to a child. He looks at the picture which is facing up and says the *I WORK* rhyme naming the worker in the picture.

> ***I WORK***
> *I'm a _____ (firefighter)*
> *And I work too*
> *Name one job you think I do.*

After he says the rhyme, another child calls out something a firefighter does. The child with the cube rolls it to another child who repeats the *I WORK* rhyme changing the worker to the one which is now facing up.

Continue rolling the cube, identifying the workers and naming jobs which they might do. (When the same worker comes up again, children just think of other jobs that the worker does, such as a firefighter puts out fires, saves people's lives, washes fire trucks, etc.)

GOING SHOPPING

Have the children name a store in the community which they shop at, for example a grocery store. Tell them to think of the different workers at the grocery store. You start the game by saying, "*I am going food shopping and I'll see a _____ (baker)."* Let a child repeat the sentence and fill in a different worker. Continue until the children have named the workers that they might see in the grocery store.

Have a child name another store in the community and play the game again.

LANGUAGE GAMES

TELL A STORY

Pick a place in the community with which the children are familiar, for example a popular restaurant. Say to the children, *"Let's tell a story about going to _____ for dinner. Close your eyes and think about times when you have gone to _____ to eat. Who do you go with? What workers are there? What do you have to eat and drink? Open your eyes and let's begin."*

GOING OUT

"It's almost time for dinner. We're going to _____ to eat. Let's see who's going. (Children talk about who would go.) *Should we walk or drive?"* (Children tell how they would go. Continue developing the story.)

On other days tell more *GOING OUT* stories:
- School
- Gas station
- Library
- Grocery store
- Clothes store

WAKE UP

Tell the children to think about a worker they would like to be and keep it a secret. When they've thought of one, they should lie down for a good night sleep, because when their alarm clock goes off, they'll have to wake up for work.

Let the children sleep for awhile. Make an alarm clock sound and say, "(Child name), *it's time to wake-up and go to work. What job are you doing today?"* The child sits up and names his job. Continue until everyone is awake and ready for work.

PASS IT ON

Have the children sit in a circle. Whisper a tongue twister to a child. That child whispers it to the child next to him and so on. After it has been passed on 4-5 times, have the child say the twister aloud. Talk about the worker named in the tongue twister. Start the game again with another twister. Here are some to start with:

- A firefighter fights fires.
- A seamstress sews socks.
- A clerk counts cash.
- A baker bakes bread.
- A letter carrier lifts lots of letters.
- A custodian keeps our classroom clean.

ACTIVE GAMES

WORKER PANTOMIME

Using workers with whom the children are familiar, give the children directions and let them act out different occupations. Be sure to give the children time to really pantomime each one. Add directions to expand the acting.

- *"You are a grocer putting lots of food in a customer's grocery bag."*
- *"You are a letter carrier walking from house to house putting mail in each person's box."*
- *"You are a firefighter putting out a fire."* (The fire is out and now you must wrap up your hose.)
- *"You are a lifeguard swimming to help a person in trouble."*
- *"You are a bus driver driving the children to school."* (Remember to stop at stop signs and red lights.)

Continue.

BOOKS

VIRGINIA LEE BURTON — *MIKE MULLIGAN AND HIS STEAM SHOVEL*
ALEXANDRA DAY — *CARL GOES SHOPPING*
ANN MORRIS — *ON THE GO*

TRANSPORTATION

FOR OPENERS

TAKE A PRETEND TRIP AROUND YOUR TOWN. BEGIN THE TRIP BY SINGING THE FIRST VERSE OF *'THE WHEELS ON THE BUS.'* (SEE FINGERPLAYS.) AFTER SINGING SAY, *"FIRST STOP, THE LIBRARY. EVERYONE OUT AND WE'LL CHOOSE BOOKS FOR THE CLASSROOM. (TALK ABOUT THE LIBRARY.) ALL ABOARD FOR THE NEXT STOP."* SING *'THE WHEELS ON THE BUS'* AGAIN AND THEN SAY, *"SECOND STOP,"* (CHILD NAMES A PLACE). DISCUSS THAT PLACE. CONTINUE YOUR DRIVE UNTIL YOU'VE BEEN ALL AROUND YOUR TOWN.

FINGERPLAYS

WHEELS ON THE BUS

The wheels on the bus go 'round and 'round,
'Round and 'round, 'round and 'round.
The wheels on the bus go 'round and 'round,
All through the town.

The people on the bus go up and down,
Up and down, up and down.
The people on the bus go up and down,
All through the town.

The money on the bus goes clink, clink, clink,
Clink, clink, clink.
The money on the bus goes clink, clink, clink,
All through the town.

The driver on the bus says, "Move on back," etc.

The children on the bus say, "Yak, yak, yak," etc.

The mothers on the bus say, "Sh, sh, sh," etc.

The wipers on the bus go swish, swish, swish, etc.

The horn on the bus goes honk, honk, honk, etc.

The wheels on the bus go 'round and 'round,
'Round and 'round, 'round and 'round.
The wheels on the bus go 'round and 'round,
All through the town.

OCCUPATIONS

FINGERPLAYS

MOTOR BOAT

Motor boat, motor boat
Go so fast!
Motor boat, motor boat
Step on the gas!
Vrrmmm, vrrmmm.

THE TRAIN

This is a train
Puffing down the track.
Now it's going forward,
Now it's going back.

Now the bell is ringing,
Now the whistle blows.
What a lot of noise it makes
Everywhere it goes.

THE FREIGHT TRAIN

Here is the engine on the track;
Here is the coal car, just in back;

Here is the boxcar to carry the freight;
Here is the mail car. Don't be late!

Way back here at the end of the train
Rides the caboose through the sun and the rain.

SNACK

CELERY TRUCKS
YOU'LL NEED
Celery
Soft cheese
Olive slices

TO MAKE: Clean the celery and cut it into 3" pieces. Let the children stuff each one with soft cheese and then make them into trucks by adding olive slice steering wheels.

FIELD TRIPS

● On a nice day sit on the sidewalk and watch the vehicles go by. As each passes by, point and call out what it is.

LANGUAGE GAMES

WHAT DO I DO?

Get a variety of model vehicles — truck, car, fire engine, police car, motorcycle, horse, boat, plane, bus, etc. Put them in a bag.

Pass the bag to a child and have him pull out a vehicle. Keeping it a secret, he should look at it and then move as if he were it. The other children name the vehicle and then discuss what workers would drive it.

AIR, LAND, OR WATER

Make lots of transportation cards by cutting out magazine pictures of different land, water, and space vehicles and gluing them to index cards. Cover 3 shoe boxes, leaving the top and bottom separate. Draw a cloud on one, land on the second, and water on the third. Cut a slit in the top of each one.

Bring the cards and boxes to circle time. Set the boxes in a row so that the children can easily see them. Pass out the cards. Have a child hold up his card and the others call out what it is. Then the child should drop it in the appropriate box. Continue in this manner until all of the cards have been sorted into the boxes.

PARKING LOT

Get 7 different model vehicles. Make a parking lot by cutting a piece of posterboard into an 8"x28" strip. Divide the board into 7 equal spaces.

Bring the board and vehicles to circle time. Pass out the vehicles to the children. Have the children drive them to the lot and park them. After the vehicles have been parked, point to each one and name it.

Have the children cover their eyes. You drive one of the vehicles away. Have the children open their eyes and guess which vehicle has been driven off to work. Continue until all of the vehicles have left the parking lot.

OCCUPATIONS

LANGUAGE GAMES

COMPARE AND CONTRAST

Hold up pictures or models of two vehicles. Have the children look at them carefully and find all of the things which are the same. Look at the vehicles again and name the things which are different. Repeat with pictures/models of other vehicles.

PEEK-A-BOO

Make a *PEEK-A-BOO PAD* and *CARDS* —

PEEK-A-BOO PAD: Get 6 pieces of construction paper. In the middle of the first sheet cut a one inch circle. Continue with the other pieces, cutting a 3" circle in the second, a 5" in the third, a 7" in the fourth, a 9" in the fifth, and no circle in the last one (back page).

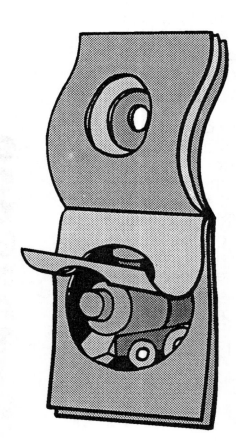

THE CARDS: Get a variety of large transportation pictures. Glue each one to a piece of 9"x12" construction paper.

Assemble the PAD by staggering the pages so that they are offset at the top by about an 1/8" with the top page the highest. Tape them together on the backside.

Bring the *PEEK-A-BOO PAD* and *CARDS* to circle time. Secretly slip one vehicle card in front of the last page and hold it up for the children to see. Tell them to look carefully. You might walk around so that they can get an even closer look. *"What do you see?"* (Discuss.) *"Can you guess what the picture might be?"* (Discuss.) Flip the page. *"Now what do you see?"* (Discuss.) *"Can you tell what vehicle it is yet?"*

Continue flipping pages, talking about the clues and predicting what vehicle is pictured. At the end look at the whole picture. Were your predictions correct? Slip another *CARD* into the *PAD* and play *PEEK-A-BOO* again.

LANGUAGE GAMES

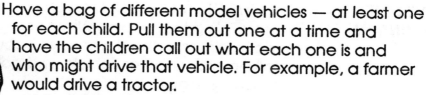

VEHICLE HUNT

Have a bag of different model vehicles — at least one for each child. Pull them out one at a time and have the children call out what each one is and who might drive that vehicle. For example, a farmer would drive a tractor.

After talking about each vehicle say to the children, *"I want you to watch me carefully. I am going to park each vehicle in a parking space somewhere in the room. You remember where each one is."* (While the children watch, park the vehicles on shelves, chairs, and so forth either a few each time or all of them at once.)

Now say to the group, *"Farmer Irroyo (child's name) is going to work. Can anyone help him find his tractor?"* After someone names a place he thinks it's parked, Farmer Irroyo goes and gets his tractor and drives it back to the circle time area. Continue until all of the workers have found their vehicles and are off to work.

VARIATION:

Let the children park the vehicles rather than you.

ACTIVE GAMES

RED LIGHT, GREEN LIGHT

Make transportation cards by using magazine pictures and gluing them to pieces of construction paper. Put the cards in a box.

Have all of the children stand at one end of the room with the parking lot at the other end. Pass the box to a child, have him pull out one transportation card, and tell the others what it is. You go to the parking lot.

When you say, *"Green light"* all of the children should start their engines and begin driving the named vehicle toward you. When you say, "Red light" they stop. Continue alternating `green light' and `red light' until all of the children have parked their vehicles in the lot. Begin again with a different vehicle.

189

ACTIVE GAMES

OVER THE MOUNTAIN

Sing *THE TRAIN CHUGGED OVER THE MOUNTAIN* while pretending to be trains. When you get over the mountain, talk about where you could go. After talking pick another vehicle and go over the mountain again.

THE TRAIN CHUGGED OVER THE MOUNTAIN
(tune: The Bear Went Over the Mountain)

The train chugged over the mountain,
The train chugged over the mountain,
The train chugged over the mountain,
To see where it should go.

To see where it should go,
To see where it should go,
The train chugged over the mountain,
To see where it should go.

Continue:

- *The boat paddled over the mountain*
- *The plane flew over the mountain*
- *The bus drove over the mountain*

BOOKS

LAURA KRASNY BROWN AND MARC BROWN — *DINOSAUR TRAVEL*
DONALD CREWS — *FLYING*
DONALD CREWS — *SCHOOL BUS*
MARYANN KOVALSKI — *THE WHEELS ON THE BUS*
CHARLOTTE POMERANTZ — *HOW MANY TRUCKS CAN A TOW TRUCK TOW?*
DIANE SIEBERT — *TRAIN SONG*
DIANE SIEBERT — *TRUCK SONG*

HATS

FOR OPENERS

MAKE A *WORKER WHEEL*. GET A 16" PIZZA BOARD OR CUT A PIECE OF POSTERBOARD. DIVIDE THE CIRCLE INTO 6 EQUAL SECTIONS. DUPLICATE EACH HAT, COLOR IT, AND GLUE IT IN A SECTION. COVER THE BOARD WITH CLEAR ADHESIVE PAPER. MAKE A SPINNER AND FASTEN IT IN THE CENTER OF THE BOARD.

BRING THE *WORKER WHEEL* TO CIRCLE TIME. SET IT ON THE FLOOR AND FLICK THE SPINNER. HAVE A CHILD CALL OUT WHAT HAT THE SPINNER STOPPED ON. LET SOMEONE ELSE NAME THE WORKER WHO WOULD WEAR THE HAT AND ONE JOB HE OR SHE DOES. FLICK AGAIN AND CONTINUE TALKING.

OCCUPATIONS

SNACK

UPSIDE DOWN HATS
YOU'LL NEED
Oranges
Yogurt
Cinnamon

TO MAKE: Cut the oranges in half. Have the children use spoons to help scoop out the fruit. Fill each *hat* with yogurt and sprinkle it with cinnamon.

FIELD TRIPS

● Call ahead and make arrangements to visit a sports store in your community. Ask the person who gives you the tour to point out headgear that people wear when they play different sports. Have the person also explain why each hat is necessary — what happens in each sport to make the headgear protection so important.

LANGUAGE GAMES

WHO IS WALKING TO WORK?

Have the children sit in a circle. Set different worker hats and/or headbands in the middle. (football helmet, baseball cap, construction hat, cowboy hat, firefighter helmet, nurse hat, clown hat, etc.) Have the children cover their eyes. You walk around the outside of the circle and tap a child on the shoulder. That child should very quietly get up, choose a worker hat, and begin to walk around the inside of the circle. You say:

"A friend of yours is walking to work,
Open your eyes and see who it is."

The children call out the type of work the hat depicts and the child's name, such as, *"Firefighter Peggy is walking to work."* The child puts the hat back in the center and sits back down. Have the children cover their eyes again and repeat the game.

WHICH HAT DO I WEAR?

Line up a variety of worker hats so that the children can easily see them. Say a riddle about a type of worker. Have the children decide what worker you are describing and which hat that person would wear. Here are a few to begin with:

- *I use a ball in my work.*
  Sometimes I throw it and sometimes I kick it,
  I tackle other players.
  Who am I and what hat do I wear?

- *You see me at the hospital.*
  I help you when you're hurt.
  I assist the doctor.
  Who am I and what hat do I wear?

- *I use a ball in my work.*
  I throw, catch, and hit it.
  Sometimes I hit a home run.
  Who am I and what hat do I wear?

- *I use a hose and water.*
  I help you if you have a fire.
  I ride on a fire truck.
  Who am I and what hat do I wear?

OCCUPATIONS

193

ACTIVE GAMES

MUSICAL HATS   Have the children hold hands and form a large circle. Set as many worker hats as you have inside of the circle just in front of the children. (It is not necessary to have one hat for every child.)

Start the music and have the children walk around the hats. Stop the music and freeze. Those children standing in front of the hats should put them on. Start the music and continue walking. Stop the music and freeze. Give directions to certain children to take off their hats and set them on the floor. Start the music and walk. Stop the music and freeze. Give directions as to who should take off or put on hats. Continue in this manner.

HAT DANCE   Select music which the children like to dance to. Have hats for half of the children to wear. Pass out the hats. Tell the children that when you start the music they can dance whatever why they would like, but when they hear the music stop, they should `freeze.' Those who have hats should give them to children who do not. Start the music again and dance. Stop the music, freeze, and switch hats again, except this time a child cannot take a hat which he has already worn. Start the music and dance again. Each time you stop the music, switch hats trying never to wear the same one twice.

BOOKS

JOAN BLOS — *MARTIN'S HATS*
ESPHTY SLOBODKINA — *CAPS FOR SALE*

PICNICS

GET ALL OF THE PICNIC TABLE SUPPLIES - TABLECLOTH, PLATES, PLASTIC TABLEWARE, SALT AND PEPPER, CUPS, EMPTY KETCHUP AND MUSTARD CONTAINERS, NAPKINS, AND SO ON.

LAY THE TABLECLOTH IN THE MIDDLE OF YOUR CIRCLE TIME AREA AND SET IT FOR YOUR PICNIC. HAVE THE CHILDREN LOOK AT IT CAREFULLY AND THEN COVER THEIR EYES. ADD, SUBTRACT OR MOVE SOMETHING ON THE TABLE. HAVE THE CHILDREN UNCOVER THEIR EYES AND LOOK FOR THE CHANGE WHILE SINGING `SILLY PICNIC TABLE.' AFTER SINGING TALK ABOUT THE CHANGE. PLAY OVER AND OVER.

SILLY PICNIC TABLE
(TUNE: FRERE JACQUES - last 2 lines)
SILLY PICNIC TABLE, SILLY PICNIC TABLE
I KNOW WHAT'S WRONG, I KNOW WHAT'S WRONG.

FINGERPLAYS

DAY AT THE BEACH

Ocean breeze blowing,
Feet kick and splash,
Ocean waves breaking
On rocks with a crash.

Children finding seashells,
Children sifting sand,
Friends building castles
As high as they can.

I stretch my arms out
As far as they'll reach.
Oh, my what fun
On this picnic at the beach.

PICNIC BUG

1, 2, 3 there's a bug on me.
Where did he go?
I don't know.

PICNIC TREATS

Will you have a cookie,
Or a piece of pie,
Or a big juicy hot dog?
Well, so will I.

RECREATION

SNACK

PICNIC PUNCH
YOU'LL NEED
6 ounce can frozen lemonade concentrate
6 ounce can frozen limeade concentrate
1 cup water
1 liter bottle chilled gingerale
Ice (optional)

TO MAKE: Thaw concentrates. Blend them well with a cup of water. Add the gingerale and stir gently to blend. Serve over ice if you wish.

LANGUAGE GAMES

PICNIC PUZZLES

Find magazine pictures of different picnic foods, cut them out and glue them to construction paper. Cut each picture in half using a straight, curved, or zig-zag line. Tie a rope between 2 chairs.

Pass one piece from each of the picnic puzzles to different children; you keep the other pieces. Clip one puzzle piece to the clothesline. Have the children look at their pieces. The child who has the other half of the puzzle should come up and clip it to the rope next to the first piece. Does it fit? Continue until all of the *PICNIC PUZZLES* are together.

IF

Pretend that you are going on a picnic and you need to make a list of what to bring. Say to the children, *"If I were going on a picnic, I'd bring a _____.* (frisbee) Everyone says, *"If I were going on a picnic, I'd bring a frisbee and a _____.* (Call on a child to name one more thing, such as a thermos.) Everyone says, *"If I were going on a picnic, I'd bring a frisbee, a thermos, and a _____.* (Call on a third child.) Continue in this manner until you're ready for the picnic.

YES OR NO

Spread a picnic blanket or tablecloth in the circle time area and have the children sit around it pretending to be at a picnic. Ask questions about picnics which the children can answer *"yes"* or *"no."* These will get you started:

● *"We eat hot dogs at picnics."*
● *"We play softball at picnics."*
● *"Lions visit us on picnics."*
● *"We toss balloons at picnics."*
● *"We sit on blankets at picnics."*

Continue.

196

ACTIVE GAMES

ROPE GAMES

Bring a clothesline to circle time.

- **Higher-Lower:** You and a child sit on the floor and hold the rope taut. Have the others take turns coming up to the rope and saying, *"Higher"* if they want you to raise the rope up or *"Lower"* if they want you to put it closer to the ground. Then the child jumps over the rope. Continue until the children have had several opportunities.

- **Snake:** You and a child sit on the floor and wiggle the rope side to side so that it moves like a snake. Each child comes up to the snake and says either, *"Wiggle faster, snake"* or *"Wiggle slower, snake."* The snake speeds up or slows down and the child jumps over it.

- **Over-Under:** You and a child stand and hold the rope taut. Each child comes up to the rope and you tell him to go over or under the rope. Then the child decides if he wants the rope higher or lower. You move it as he directs and then he crosses it.

- **Swing:** You and a child stand and swing the rope gently. The children leap across as it is moving.

BOOKS

JIMMY KENNEDY — *THE TEDDY BEARS PICNIC*
ROBERT WELBER — *THE WINTER PICNIC*

TOYS

FOR OPENERS

HAVE THE CHILDREN STAND UP. TOSS EACH OF THEM AN INVISIBLE BALL. AFTER EVERYONE HAS CAUGHT HIS BALL START TELLING THE CHILDREN HOW TO USE IT, FIRST INDIVIDUALLY, THEN WITH ONE OTHER PERSON, AND FINALLY WITH THE WHOLE GROUP.

INDIVIDUALLY

- *"HOLD YOUR BALL TIGHTLY IN BOTH HANDS."*
- *"BALANCE YOUR BALL IN ONE HAND - THE OTHER HAND."*
- *"TOSS YOUR BALL HIGH IN THE AIR AND CATCH IT."*
- *"DRIBBLE YOUR BALL"*
- *"DRIBBLE YOUR BALL AND SHOOT A BASKET."*

WITH ANOTHER PERSON

- *"AMANDA, TOSS YOUR BALL TO GINGER."* (KEEP NAMING PAIRS.)
- *"SAMIE, KICK YOUR BALL TO A FRIEND."* (CONTINUE NAMING CHILDREN.)
- *"BOUNCE YOUR BALL TO THE PERSON I TELL YOU TO."* (NAME CHILDREN.)

IN A GROUP

- *"PUT ALL OF THE BALLS ON THE FLOOR."*
- *"PASS ONE BALL AROUND THE CIRCLE. I'LL START."*
- *"KICK THE BALL AROUND THE CIRCLE."* (NAME CHILD TO START.)
- *"PASS THE BALL AROUND THE CIRCLE BETWEEN YOUR HEADS. I'LL START"*

FINGERPLAYS

MY SAND BOX

On sunny days I go to play,
In a magic land not far away.
It's filled with sand for castles fair
Or streets that go just everywhere.

And in my truck the sand I load
To fill a hole just down the road.
To find the place is not too hard
It's out the door in my back yard.
   Dick Wilmes

I AM A TOP

I am a top all wound up tight;
I whirl and whirl with all my might;
And now the whirls are out of me
So I will rest as still as can be.

I'M BOUNCING

I'm bouncing, bouncing everywhere.
I bounce and bounce into the air.
I'm bouncing, bouncing like a ball.
I bounce and bounce, then down I fall.

SNACK

CORNFLAKE BALLS
YOU'LL NEED
1 cup peanut butter
1/2 cup honey
31/2 cup cornflakes

TO MAKE: Stir the peanut butter and honey in a small pot over medium heat until blended. Add the cornflakes. Chill the dough for 30 minutes, roll into balls and enjoy with a glass of milk.

LANGUAGE GAMES

TOYLAND

Using a toy catalogue cut out 8-10 pictures of popular toys. Glue each picture to an index card. Turn them face down in the middle of your circle time area. Use the cards to tell a story about TOYLAND.

You could begin the story by saying something like this:

TOYLAND

"Jamal was so excited because today he and his mom were going to the toy store to look at all of the toys. They always have a good time looking. When they walked into the store the first toy they saw was _____. (Have a child turn over a card and let him continue telling the story using the picture he picked.)

199

LANGUAGE GAMES

TOY CONCENTRATION

Using toy catalogues, cut out pairs of different toys and glue each picture to an unlined index card - at least one for each child. Bring them to circle time and pass them out to the children. Let each child hold up his card/s, name the toy/s, and then put it face down in the middle of the area.

After all of the cards are down, have 2 children go to the cards. Have one child turn a card over. Have the second child turn another card over. If the cards match, pick up the pair and give it to you; if not, turn the cards back over. Play until all of the cards have been paired.

I WENT TO THE STORE

Have one child begin the game by saying, "*I went to the Toy Store and bought a _____.*" The next child continues, "*I went to the Toy Store and bought a _____ and a _____.*" Continue, always repeating the previous toys and then naming another one. Keep adding toys as long as you can, then stop. Start over by saying, "*Later that day I went back to the Toy Store and bought a _____.*" Continue.

IMAGINATION STRETCHER

Cup your hands to make an imaginary small box. Say to the children, "*I wonder what toy is in this small box? (Open your hands just a little and take a peek.) Oh, I'll give you clues to help you guess what it is.*" Give clues until the children know what toy is in your imaginary box. Cup your hands (maybe your arms) again making a different size box. Play again.

LISTEN CAREFULLY

Say the first syllable of a toy, such as "*puz.*" Let the children finish the word "*puzzle.*" If the toy word is only one syllable say the beginning sound, such as, "*tr.*" Let the children name toys that begin with that sound - truck, train, etc.

ACTIVE GAMES

BOUNCING BALLS
Have the children stand in a circle, hold hands, and form a giant bouncing ball. Give directions to the ball.
- "*Bouncing ball, bounce up high.*" (Stop)
- "*Bouncing ball, bounce fast.*" (Stop)
- "*Bouncing ball, bounce to the wall.*" (Stop)
- "*Bouncing ball, bounce in slow motion.*" (Stop)
- Continue
- Last command - "*Bouncing ball, bounce slower, slower, slower. Sit on the shelf.*"

JACK IN THE BOX
Have the children squat down in the `boxes` and listen carefully as you give them directions to stay in their `boxes` or come out.
- "*Jack and Jill in the box.*" (Squat, hands over head.)
- "*Jack and Jill in the box.*" (Stay in)
- "*Jack and Jill jump out of your box.*" (Jump out)
- "*Jack and Jill in the box.*" (Squat)
- "*Jack and Jill fly out of your box.*" (Fly around)
- "*Jack and Jill in the box.*" (Squat)
- "*Jack and Jill in the box.*" (Stay in)
- Continue - leap, hop, skip, etc.

BOOKS

DON FREEMAN — *CORDUROY*
MICHAEL GREEN — *THE VELVETEEN RABBIT*
CROCKETT JOHNSON — *HAROLD AND THE PURPLE CRAYON*
MARGARET REY ·– *CURIOUS GEORGE FLIES A KITE*
CHARLOTTE ZOI OTOW — *WILLIAM'S DOLL*

RECREATION

PARADES

FOR OPENERS

TELL THE CHILDREN A STORY ABOUT A TOWN PARADE. AS YOU TELL ABOUT THE VARIOUS ANIMALS, VEHICLES, AND PEOPLE IN THE PARADE, STOP AND LET THE CHILDREN FILL IN THE PARADE SOUNDS. YOU COULD BEGIN:

TOWN PARADE

MY FAMILY WAS VERY EXCITED, FOR OUR TOWN PARADE WAS TODAY. WE GOT DRESSED VERY QUICKLY, ATE BREAKFAST, AND THEN WALKED OVER TO THE PLACE WHERE THE PARADE WOULD BEGIN. SOON THE BAND STARTED TO PLAY, AND THE PARADE WAS OFF. FIRST I HEARD THE HORNS. (LET CHILDREN `PLAY' HORNS.) *NEXT CAME THE BIG DRUMS. THEY WERE LOUD.* (CHILDREN `PLAY' DRUMS.) *BEHIND THE DRUMS WERE THE CYMBALS.* (CHILDREN `PLAY' CYMBALS.) *AFTER THE FIRST BAND PASSED, A CLOWN TROUPE CAME DOWN THE STREET RIDING MOTORCYCLES.* (CHILDREN PRETEND THEY ARE RIDING MOTORCYCLES.)

CONTINUE IN THIS MANNER ALWAYS PAUSING TO ENJOY THE SOUNDS IN YOUR TOWN PARADE.

- POLICE CAR SIRENS
- HORSE CLIPPETY-CLOP
- DECORATED CARS HONK
- FIRE ENGINE SIRENS
- CLOWNS BLOW WHISTLE
- SOLDIERS MARCH

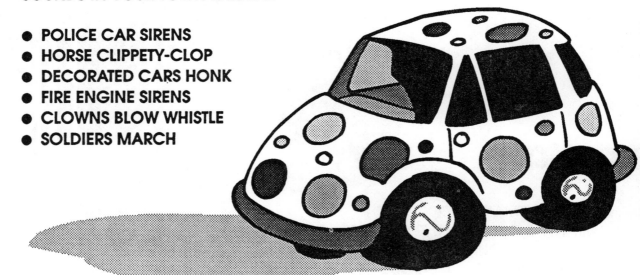

FINGERPLAYS

PARADE CLOWNS

Sometimes I am tall.
Sometimes I am small.
Sometimes I am very, very, tall.
Sometimes I am very, very, small.
Sometimes tall, sometimes small,
See how I am now.

MARCH ALONG
(tune: Row, Row, Row Your Boat)

March, march, march along
Our legs go up and down.
Marching, marching, marching,
 marching
All around the town.
  Liz Wilmes

PARADE ELEPHANT

Right foot, left foot, see me go.
I am gray and big and slow.
I come walking down the street
With my trunk and four big feet.

DRUMS

Boom! Boom! Boom!
Goes the big brass drum.
Rat-a-tat-tat goes the little one.

And down the street in line we come
To the boom, boom, boom of the
 big brass drum,
And the rat-a-tat-tat of the little one.

TOWN PARADE

The people are beside the street,
All standing in the sun.
I hear the noon whistle blowing,
The parade has just begun.

Finally comes the last police car,
The music starts to fade.
We had a nice afternoon,
Watching the town parade.

(Say the first verse, talk about
parades, and then say the last
verse.)
  Dick Wilmes

SNACK

GOING BANANAS
YOU'LL NEED:
1 banana for every 3-4 children
Carob syrup
Crushed graham crackers

TO MAKE: Peel the bananas and cut each one into 3 or 4 pieces. Stick a
popsicle stick into each piece. Dip the banana into the syrup and roll it in
crushed graham crackers. Lay the popsicles on a tray and freeze.

RECREATION

CLASSROOM VISITOR

● Invite parents who have marched in parades to come into the classroom and tell the children what it was like. If they wore a costume or have photographs ask them to bring these items along.

LANGUAGE GAMES

MIXED UP STORY Start telling a parade story. As you tell it have the children listen carefully. Purposely make mistakes, such as having the wrong sequence of events, or parade animals, vehicles, and people doing inappropriate actions, and/or telling about activities which are non-parade related. When the children hear a mistake, have them hold out their hands in a `stop signal.' Ask, "What's wrong?" Let them tell you and then continue your story.

PARADE SWITCH Gather 4-10 models of different people, animals, and vehicles that would be in a parade. (Clown, police officer, firefighter, horse, dog, truck, ambulance, etc.)
Line them up as if in a parade. Touch each one and have the children call out who/what it is. Have the children cover their eyes. Switch 2 of the parade goers. Have the children uncover their eyes and look at the parade again. What did you switch? Put the parade back to its original line-up and play again.

LISTEN CAREFULLY

Get 2-4 examples of several different musical instruments which people play in a parade - drums, triangles, maracas, sticks, etc. Keep one of each type of instrument out of sight in a box. Pass the rest of the instruments to the children. (Some may have duplicates.)
Without letting the children see, play one of the instruments. The children who think they have the matching instrument should play theirs. After the children have played, bring your intrument out, play it again, and see if the instruments match. Everybody clap. Have each child pass his instrument to his neighbor. Have the children try out their new instruments and play *LISTEN CAREFULLY* again.

ACTIVE GAMES

PARADE MARSHALL SAYS

Talk about parades with the children - what happens, who's in them, what the people do, and so on.

After talking have the children pretend that they are in a parade. You be the Parade Marshall giving the directions:

- "Parade Marshall says, `Blow your horns.' Stop."
- "Parade Marshall says, `Drive your motorcycles.' Stop."
- "Parade Marshall says, `Twirl your batons.' Stop."
- "Parade Marshall says, `Drive your floats.' Stop."
- Continue
- Last direction - "Parade Marshall says, `The parade is over. Clap for our good time.' "

HAVE A PARADE

Get several Sousa Marches. Pass out scarves and streamers to the children. Have the children get eady to march, start the music, and *HAVE A PARADE.*

REPEAT THE BEAT

Have a drum or 2 rhythm sticks. At first have the children sit down. Begin beating a rhythm. Have the children march with their arms. Stop and the children freeze. Begin beating a different rhythm and have the children start marching their arms to the new rhythm

Now have the children stand up. Start beating a rhythm and leading the parade around the room. Stop beating and freeze. Change the rhythm and continue the parade marching to the beat of the new rhythm.

BOOKS

ED EMBERLY — *PARADE BOOK*
PETER SPIER — *CRASH! BANG! BOOM!*

HAPPY BIRTHDAY

FOR OPENERS

CUT AT LEAST ONE 2"x6" CONSTRUCTION PAPER STRIP FOR EACH CHILD. DURING FREE CHOICE GIVE ALL OF THE CHILDREN THE OPPORTUNITY TO DICTATE MESSAGES TO THE BIRTHDAY CHILD. WRITE EACH ONE ON A SEPARATE STRIP.

BRING THE MESSAGES TO CIRCLE TIME AND HAVE EACH CHILD `READ' HIS MESSAGE/S TO THE BIRTHDAY CHILD. YOU STAPLE THE STRIPS TOGETHER, MESSAGE SIDE OUT, AFTER EACH ONE IS `READ.' HANG THE BIRTHDAY CHAIN IN A SPECIAL PLACE AND THEN LET THE CHILD TAKE IT HOME.

FINGERPLAYS

THANK YOU
(Stand with the birthday child and say the rhyme together)

My hands say thank you
With a clap, clap, clap.

My feet say thank you
With a tap, tap, tap.

Clap! Clap! Clap!
Tap! Tap! Tap!

Turn myself around and bow.
Thank you, everyone.

SNACK

THUMB PRINT COOKIES
YOU'LL NEED:
2 cups flour
1 t salt
2/3 cup oil
4-5 T water
Peanut butter to
fill thumbprints

TO MAKE: Mix the first four ingredients together, using a fork. Roll the dough into small balls, pressing a thumbprint in each one. Bake them on a greased cookie sheet for 8-10 minutes at 400°. Let cool and fill with peanut butter.

CLASSROOM VISITOR

● On each child's birthday invite his/her family to join the class for the day or a specific part of one, such as circle time/snack. While visiting, have the parent tell the class about the birthday child when s/he was younger. Maybe the parent has a baby picture to show the children.

LANGUAGE GAMES

SPECIAL BOOK — Encourage the Birthday Child to bring a special book on his birthday for you to read to the group.

BIRTHDAY PARTY — Using the Birthday Child's name, let the children help you tell a story about a birthday party. You begin the story and then let the children add their thoughts and ideas.

BIRTHDAY PARTY

Today is Samantha's birthday. (How old are you Samantha?) Yes, she is 5 years old. She is going to have a party. At her party she is going to play games, have a cake, and open presents. The first game the children will play is _____. (Let children respond.) Continue the story.

ACTIVE GAMES

BIRTHDAY CLAP AND TAP — Let the Birthday Child lead the group in BIRTHDAY CLAP AND TAP. He sits where everyone can easily see him and begins clapping his hands together. Everyone follows him. When he wants to, he stops clapping his hands and starts tapping his thighs. Everyone follows him. He continues clapping and tapping in different ways with everyone copying his moves. At the end, clap loudly for the Birthday Child and sing "Happy Birthday."

HUG TAG — The Birthday Child is *IT*. Everyone runs. (Walks fast if inside.) *IT* chases the children. When he catches someone he gives him a hug. That person becomes IT, catches someone, and hugs him, who then becomes IT. Continue for several more times and then stop for a rest. Play again and again with the Birthday Child starting each time.

BOOKS

NORMAN BRIDWELL — *CLIFFORD'S BIRTHDAY PARTY*
ERIC CARLE — *THE SECRET BIRTHDAY MESSAGE*
PAT HUTCHIN'S — *HAPPY BIRTHDAY, SAM*
EZRA JACK KEATS — *A LETTER TO AMY*
MERLE PEEK — *MARY WORE HER RED DRESS AND HENRY WORE HIS GREEN SNEAKERS*

RECREATION

CLOWNS

FOR OPENERS

CUT OUT A HUGE CLOWN SHAPE (PETE) FROM BUTCHER PAPER, ALONG WITH LOTS OF LARGE DOTS AND PATCHES FROM COLORED CONSTRUCTION PAPER.

BRING PETE AND THE PATCHES TO CIRCLE TIME. INTRODUCE HIM TO THE CHILDREN AND TELL THEM THAT PETE NEEDS HELP GETTING HIS PATCHES ARRANGED. HOLD UP EACH PATCH AND HAVE THE CHILDREN CALL OUT THE COLOR AND THEN SET IT NEXT TO PETE. HAVE A CHILD COME UP, PICK A PATCH, AND SET IT ON PETE. CONTINUE HAVING CHILDREN PICK PATCHES AND PUT THEM WHEREVER THEY WANT ON PETE.

AFTER CIRCLE TIME HAVE THOSE WHO WANT HELP YOU GLUE THE PATCHES DOWN. CARRY *PATCHWORK PETE TO* THE ART AREA. LET THE CHILDREN USE COLORED MARKERS TO DRAW STITCHES AROUND EACH OF THE PATCHES. HANG PETE AT THE CHILDREN'S EYE LEVEL ON YOUR CLASSROOM DOOR.

FINGERPLAYS

WHO FEELS HAPPY?

Who feels happy this sunny day?
All who do, clap their hands and sway.

Who feels happy this sunny day?
All who do nod their heads and sway.

Who feels happy this sunny day?
All who do tap their shoulders and sway.

FINGERPLAYS

STAND UP TALL

Stand up tall
Hands in the air;
Now sit down
And growl like a bear.

Clap your hands;
Make a frown.
Smile and smile,
And flop like a clown!

THIS LITTLE CLOWN

This little clown is silly and fat;
This little clown does tricks with a cat.

This little clown sings a funny song;
This little clown is tall and strong.

This little clown is wee and small,
But he does tricks with a great big ball.

I WISH I WERE A CIRCUS CLOWN

I wish I were a circus clown,
With smile so wide and eyes so round,
With pointed hat and funny nose,
And polka dots upon my clothes.

SNACK

CLOWN NOSES

YOU'LL NEED:
2 envelopes unflavored gelatin
4 cups cranberry juice

TO MAKE: In sauce pan, bring 2 cups of juice to boil. Pour the gelatin in a bowl and slowly stir in hot juice. Stir until all gelatin is dissolved. Add 2 cups of cold juice and stir. Pour into a pan and refrigerate until firm. Using a mellon-ball scoop, make Clown Noses for everyone.

LANGUAGE GAMES

WHO'S MISSING ?   Ask 3-5 children to stand together and make clown faces. Have the others look at the clowns and then cover their eyes. Tap one clown on the shoulder who tiptoes away and hides. The other clowns continue to make their faces. The children uncover their eyes and guess who's missing. If they guess who it is, the missing clown comes bouncing back; if not, the clown stays hidden and the children keep guessing. Play again and again with other groups of clowns.

WHAT AM I DOING?   Bring a large picture of a clown/s to circle time. Have the children look closely at the picture and talk about what the clown/s is doing. (Discuss.) Encourage more discussion by asking questions like, *"What do you think the clown will do next? Why? Do you think this clown likes to do _____?"* (Name an activity such as do somersaults.)

209

LANGUAGE GAMES

CLOWN FACES

Have the children pair up and sit facing each other. Walk around the circle and tap one child from each pair on the head, saying *"Clown"* as you do. Have the clowns cover their faces with their hands and make a clown face. While the clowns are making their faces, the others say the *CLOWN FACES* rhyme. As they finish the second line the clowns show their partners their silly faces. (Laugh and giggle.) Switch roles and play again. Change partners and continue.

CLOWN FACES

Make a smile or a frown.
Show me the face of your clown.

CLOWN PUZZLE

Duplicate and color the pieces to the clown puzzle. Back each piece with felt/magnet tape. Bring the pieces and the felt/magnet board to circle time.

Put the pieces in mixed up order on the left side of the board. Start putting the puzzle together by taking the clown's head and moving it to the right side of the board. Ask, *"Who sees the piece that goes on top of the clown's head?"* (Child adds that piece.) Continue until the CLOWN PUZZLE is together.

LITTLE CLOWNS

Before circle time draw a simple clown face on each finger/thumb of one hand. Introduce your finger puppets to the children.

Call on a child to name how many clowns he would like to see, such as 4. Hold up your fist and say the *LITTLE CLOWNS* rhyme. After you've played the game once, have the children participate, pretending that their fingers/thumbs are *LITTLE CLOWNS*. Change the number each time you say it.

LITTLE CLOWNS

Four little clowns stand up tall
1, 2, 3, 4. (Hold fingers up as you count.)
Four little clowns tumble and fall
4, 3, 2, 1, 0. (Tuck fingers into your fist.)

DRAW A CLOWN

Bring a large sheet of butcher paper/newsprint and different colored markers to circle time. Tack the paper to a wall. Say to the children, *"I want to draw a funny clown, but I need your help. You tell me what the clown looks like and I'll draw."* As the children tell you each part of the clown, draw it. Keep going until the clown is complete. Hang it in the room at the children's eye level.

ACTIVE GAMES

CLOWN TRICKS   Have the children stand in a circle. You start walking stiff legged, as if you were on stilts, around the outside of the circle. Tap a child on the shoulder to become the clown. He goes into the middle and the group sings *I'M A TRICKY CLOWN*. As they are singing the last line and turning around, the clown starts doing a silly movement and the children follow him. After everyone has done the movement, the clown walks around the outside of the circle, taps a new clown, and the game continues.

I'M A TRICKY CLOWN
(tune: I'm a Little Teapot)
I'm a little clown who's short and fat,
Here is my tummy, here is my hat.
I can do a trick as you will see,
Just turn around and look at me.
   Dick Wilmes

BOOKS

TOMIE DE PAOLA — *SING, PIEROT, SING*

STUFFED ANIMALS

FOR OPENERS

BRING A VERY SMALL TEDDY BEAR TO CIRCLE TIME. HAVE THE CHILDREN SIT IN A CIRCLE. ASK ONE CHILD TO LEAVE THE ROOM. (ADULT GO WITH.) GIVE THE TEDDY BEAR TO A CHILD AND ASK HIM TO HIDE IT IN HIS LAP AND START GROWLING VERY QUIETLY.

HAVE THE CHILD RETURN AND LISTEN FOR TEDDY BEAR'S GROWL. WHEN THE CHILD THINKS HE KNOWS WHERE TEDDY BEAR IS, HE SHOULD GO OVER TO THE CHILD. IF HE IS RIGHT, THE CHILD GIVES TEDDY BEAR TO HIM; IF NOT, THE CHILD WITH TEDDY BEAR GROWLS A LITTLE LOUDER. AFTER HE FINDS TEDDY BEAR, EVERYONE CLAP. SWITCH PLAYERS AND PLAY AGAIN.

ON OTHER DAYS, BRING A DIFFERENT SMALL ANIMAL AND ENJOY THE GAME AGAIN WITH NEW SOUNDS.

FINGERPLAYS

BUNNY

Bunny's ears are floppy.
Bunny's feet are hoppy.
His fur is soft,
His nose is fluffy,
His tail is short and powder-puffy.

GOING TO BED

This little boy is going to bed.
Down on the pillow he lays his head.
He wraps himself in the covers tight,
And sleeps with his teddy bear all through the night.

TEN LITTLE ELEPHANTS

One little, two little, three little elephants,
Four little, five little, six little elephants,
Seven little, eight little, nine little elephants,
Ten little elephants snuggle up tight.

RECREATION

SNACKS

TEDDY BEAR COOKIES

YOU'LL NEED
1 egg
1/2 cup melted shortening
3/4 cup honey
1/2 t cinnamon
1-2 T milk
1 t lemon juice
2 cups sifted flour
1 t baking powder

TO MAKE: Break the egg into a large bowl. Add shortening, honey, cinnamon, milk, and lemon juice. Beat until smooth. Sift the flour and baking soda together and add to the above mixture. Mix thoroughly. Roll out the dough on a floured surface. The dough should be 1/8" to 1/4" thick. Flour the teddy bear cookie cutters and cut out the cookies. Bake at 375 degrees for 9-12 minutes.

LANGUAGE GAMES

OVER THE MOUNTAIN

Teach your children the first verse of the traditional song, *THE BEAR WENT OVER THE MOUNTAIN.* After singing it, have a child name one thing that the bear might have seen. Sing again and have a second child name the first thing that the bear saw and add a second one. Continue singing and naming each thing the bear saw and adding one more until the list gets too long.

Have a child name another stuffed animal, substitute that animal in the song, and play again.

THE BEAR WENT OVER THE MOUNTAIN

The bear went over the mountain
The bear went over the mountain
The bear went over the mountain
To see what he could see.

And all that he could see was _____.

LISTEN CAREFULLY

Have several stuffed animals, such as a lion, rabbit, and skunk. Ask a child to be the Lion Tamer and leave the room. (Adult go along.) Have a second child hide the lion someplace in the room. When the Lion Tamer returns, tell him that the *Lion* escaped from his cage and must find it. Everyone will help him by roaring loudly as he gets closer to where the lion is hiding and more softly as he gets further away from the lion. Keep playing until the Lion Tamer finds his lion. Play again with the other animals.

LANGUAGE GAMES

WHO'S MISSING? Have a blanket and 7-8 stuffed animals. Tuck each animal into bed leaving its head showing. As you're saying, *"Good night"* to each animal have the children name it. After tucking the last one into bed, have the children cover their eyes. Take one of the animals out of bed and put it behind you to get a drink of water. Have the children uncover their eyes, look at the sleeping animals, and call out which one is getting a drink of water. Continue playing until all of the animals are out of bed getting their drinks.

WHO AM I? Find pictures of stuffed animals. Glue them to pieces of construction paper. Cut each one into 3 or 4 pieces so that each piece is a recognizable part of the animal. Back each piece with felt or magnet tape.

Bring the pieces and your felt/magnet board to circle time. Choose the pieces to one animal. As you say a riddle about him, put the appropriate piece on your board. For example:

- *I have long ears.* (Put ears on board.)
- *I have a friendly face.* (Face)
- *I have a furry body.* (Rest of animal)
- *Who am I?* (Name animal)

IMAGINATION STRETCHERS Have 4 or 5 stuffed animals sitting in a big vehicle. Pose different situations to the children about the animals. Here are some to begin with:

- *"What would you do if Teddy Bear had a cold?"*
- *"Teddy Bear and Giraffe want to go out and play. Where should they go? What should they do?"*
- *"Mrs. Duck wants to treat her ducklings to a surprise snack. What should she have?"*
- Continue.

WHERE'S ROVER DOG? Bring Rover Dog to circle time. Introduce him to your children. Set him in a place where the children can easily see him, such as on your lap, under a chair, on top of a shelf, etc.

Say to the children, *"Where's Rover Dog?"* Help the children be as specific as possible when they respond, such as, *"Rover Dog is sitting on your lap."* Move Rover Dog to another place and let the children respond again. After they know how to play let the children take turns putting Rover Dog in different places.

215

EXERCISES

ACTIVE GAMES

DINO DANCE Have the children pretend that they are stuffed dinosaurs. Put on dancing music and let the dinosaurs dance. Stop the music - the dinosaurs freeze in place - start the music and let the dancing continue.

BE LIKE ME Get a large stuffed animal. Tell the children to watch the animal carefully and when he moves the children should copy him.

- Animal raises and lowers one paw. (Children copy)
- Animal bows up and down, up and down.
- Animal waves both paws over his head.
- Animal spreads his legs apart and together — apart and together.
- Continue
- Last movement — Animal rests.

TEDDY BEAR EXERCISES Duplicate the EXERCISE CHART. Back it with construction paper. Bring it to circle time. Have one child be Teddy Bear. Point to one of the exercises on the chart. Teddy Bear begins to exercise and all of his friends follow him. After awhile stop and rest. Teddy Bear chooses another Teddy Bear. He comes up, you point to a second exercise, and he begins leading a second movement. Continue in this manner having different children lead *TEDDY BEAR EXERCISES.*

BOOKS

SUSANNA GRETZ — *TEDDY BEARS STAY INDOORS*
SARAH HAYES — *THIS IS BEAR*
JIMMY KENNEDY — *TEDDY BEARS PICNIC*

FOR EVERY MONTH

BUILDING BLOCKS

an activity newspaper for adults
and their young children

TAKE A LOOK AT BUILDING BLOCKS NEWSPAPER

PUBLISHED:
10 times a year including an expanded summer issue.

RATES:
   1 Year ~ $20^{00}
   2 Years ~ $36^{50}
   3 Years ~ $50^{00}
   Sample ~ $ 3^{00}

SEND YOUR NAME, ADDRESS (INCLUDING ZIP CODE), AND PAYMENT TO:

BUILDING BLOCKS
38W567 Brindlewood
Elgin, Il   60123

BUILDING BLOCKS is a 20 page early childhood activity newspaper offering a total curriculum resource to use in your classroom and share with your parents.

MONTHLY FEATURES include:

~ Reproducible parent activity calendar.

~ Activity pages highlighting language, art, physical, science/math, creative, and self/social activities which are easy to plan and implement.

~ Ready-to-use charts, games, and/or posters.

~ Special activity page for toddlers and twos.

~ Large easy-to-use illustrations.

~ 4 page **FEATURED TOPIC** *Pull-Out Section.*

BUILDING BLOCKS Library

The Circle Time Series

by Liz and Dick Wilmes. Thousands of activities for large and small groups of children. Each book is filled with Language and Active games, Fingerplays, Songs, Stories, Snacks, and more. A great resource for every library shelf.

Circle Time Book
Captures the spirit of 39 holidays and seasons.
ISBN 0-943452-00-7   **$ 12.95**

Everyday Circle Times
Over 900 ideas. Choose from 48 topics divided into 7 sections: self-concept, basic concepts, animals, foods, science, occupations, and recreation.
ISBN 0-943452-01-5   **$16.95**

More Everyday Circle Times
Divided into the same 7 sections as EVERYDAY. Features new topics such as Birds and Pizza, plus all new ideas for some popular topics contained in EVERYDAY.
ISBN 0-943452-14-7   **$16.95**

Yearful of Circle Times
52 different topics to use weekly, by seasons, or mixed throughout the year. New Friends, Signs of Fall, Snowfolk Fun, and much more.
ISBN 0-943452-10-4   **$16.95**

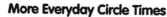

Paint Without Brushes

by Liz and Dick Wilmes. Use common materials which you already have. Discover the painting possibilities in your classroom! PAINT WITHOUT BRUSHES gives your children open-ended art activities to explore paint in lots of creative ways. A valuable art resource. One you'll want to use daily.
ISBN 0-943452-15-5   **$12.95**

Easel Art

by Liz & Dick Wilmes. Let the children use easels, walls, outside fences, clip boards, and more as they enjoy the variety of art activities filling the pages of EASEL ART. A great book to expand young children's art experiences.
ISBN 0-943452-25-2   **$ 12.95**

Everyday Bulletin Boards

by Wilmes and Moehling. Features borders, murals, backgrounds, and other open-ended art to display on your bulletin boards. Plus board ideas with patterns, which teachers can make and use to enhance their curriculum.
ISBN 0-943452-09-0   **$ 12.95**

Exploring Art

by Liz and Dick Wilmes. EXPLORING ART is divided by months. Over 250 art ideas for paint, chalk, doughs, scissors, and more. Easy to set-up in your classroom.
ISBN 0-943452-05-8   **$19.95**

CIRCLE TIME

ART

Magnet Board Fun
by Liz and Dick Wilmes. Every classroom has a magnet board, every home a refrigerator. MAGNET BOARD FUN is crammed full of games, songs, and stories. Hundreds of patterns to reproduce, color, and use immediately.
ISBN 0-943452-28-7   **$ 16.95**

Parachute Play, Revised
by Liz and Dick Wilmes. Play, wiggle, and laugh as you introduce children to the parachute. Over 150 holiday and everyday games for inside and outside play.
ISBN 0-943452-30-9   **$ 12.95**

Activities Unlimited
by Adler, Caton, and Cleveland. Hundreds of innovative activities to develop fine and gross motor skills, increase language, become self-reliant, and play cooperatively. This book will quickly become a favorite.
ISBN 0-943452-17-1   **$16.95**

Felt Board Fingerplays
by Liz and Dick Wilmes. A year full of fingerplay fun. Over 50 popular fingerplays, with full-size patterns. All accompanied by games and activities.
ISBN 0-943452-26-0   **$16.95**

Felt Board Fun
by Liz and Dick Wilmes. Make your felt board come alive. This unique book has over 150 ideas with patterns.
ISBN 0-943452-02-3   **$16.95**

Felt Board Stories
by Liz and Dick Wilmes. 25 seasonal, holiday, and any-day stories with full-size patterns. Children are involved in each story. They figure out riddles, create endings, sing with characters, add patterns, and so much more.
ISBN 0-943452-31-7   **$16.95**

Table & Floor Games
by Liz and Dick Wilmes. 32 easy-to-make, fun-to-play table/floor games with accompanying patterns ready to duplicate. Teach beginning concepts such as matching, counting, colors, alphabet, and so on.
ISBN 0-943452-16-3   **$19.95**

Learning Centers
by Liz and Dick Wilmes. Hundreds of open-ended activities to quickly involve and excite your children. You'll use it every time you plan and whenever you need a quick, additional activity. A must for every teacher's bookshelf.
ISBN 0-943452-13-9   **$19.95**

Play With Big Boxes
by Liz and Dick Wilmes. Children love big boxes. Turn them into boats, telephone booths, tents, and other play areas. Bring them to art and let children collage, build, and paint them. Use them in learning centers for games, play stages, quiet spaces, puzzles, and more, more, more.
ISBN 0-943452-23-6   **$ 12.95**

Play With Small Boxes
by Liz and Dick Wilmes. Small boxes are free, fun, and unlimited. Use them for telephones, skates, scoops, pails, doll beds, buggies, and more. So many easy activities, you'll use small boxes every day.
ISBN 0-943452-24-4   **$ 12.95**

Games for All Seasons
by Caton and Cleveland. Play with the wonder of seasons and holidays. Use acorns, pumpkins, be clouds and butterflies, go ice fishing. Over 150 learning games.
ISBN 0-943452-29-5   **$16.95**

On Track To KINDERGARTEN

by Alex Cleveland and Barb Caton.

Parents always ask: *"How can I help my child get ready for kindergarten?"* This book is the answer. The weekly activity sheets are filled with games and activities for parents to do with their children.

Available in Spanish and English.

ISBN 0-943452-32-5 (English) $14.95

ISBN 0-943452-33-3 (Spanish) $14.95

2's Experience Series

by Liz and Dick Wilmes. An exciting series developed especially for toddlers and twos!

2's-Art
Scribble, Paint, Smear, Mix, Tear, Mold, Taste, and more. Over 150 activities, plus lots of recipes and hints.
ISBN 0-943452-21-X $16.95

2's-Sensory Play
Hundreds of playful, multi-sensory activities to encourage children to look, listen, taste, touch, and smell.
ISBN 0-943452-22-8 $14.95

2's-Dramatic Play
Dress up and pretend! Hundreds of imaginary situations and settings.
ISBN 0-943452-20-1 $12.95

2's-Stories
Excite children with story books! Read—Expand the stories with games, songs, and rhymes. Over 40 books with patterns.
ISBN 0-943452-27-9 $16.95

2's-Fingerplays
A wonderful collection of easy fingerplays with accompanying games and large FINGERPLAY CARDS.
ISBN 0-943452-18-X $12.95

2's-Felt Board Fun
Make your felt board come alive. Enjoy stories, activities, and rhymes. Hundreds of extra large patterns.
ISBN 0-943452-19-8 $14.95

BUILDING BLOCKS

BUILDING BLOCKS Subscription	$20.00
CIRCLE TIME Series	
CIRCLE TIME BOOK	12.95
EVERYDAY CIRCLE TIMES	16.95
MORE EVERYDAY CIRCLE TIMES	16.95
YEARFUL OF CIRCLE TIMES	16.95
ART	
EASEL ART	12.95
EVERYDAY BULLETIN BOARDS	12.95
EXPLORING ART	19.95
PAINT WITHOUT BRUSHES	12.95
LEARNING GAMES & ACTIVITIES	
ACTIVITIES UNLIMITED	16.95
FELT BOARD FINGERPLAYS	16.95
FELT BOARD FUN	16.95
FELT BOARD STORIES	16.95
LEARNING CENTERS	19.95
MAGNET BOARD FUN	16.95
PARACHUTE PLAY, REVISED	12.95
PLAY WITH BIG BOXES	12.95
PLAY WITH SMALL BOXES	12.95
TABLE & FLOOR GAMES	19.95
ON TRACK TO KINDERGARTEN	
ENGLISH EDITION	14.95
SPANISH EDITION	14.95
2's EXPERIENCE Series	
2'S EXPERIENCE - ART	16.95
2'S EXPERIENCE - DRAMATIC PLAY	12.95
2'S EXPERIENCE - FELTBOARD FUN	14.95
2'S EXPERIENCE - FINGERPLAYS	12.95
2'S EXPERIENCE - SENSORY PLAY	14.95
2'S EXPERIENCE - STORIES	16.95

Prices subject to change without notice.

All books available from full-service book stores, educational stores, and school supply catalogs.

Check Our Website:
www.bblocksonline.com

QUALITY
BUILDING BLOCKS
SINCE 1977